D0313881

Ring Papa Ring!

The Story of An American Family

Dean Ackermann Thomson

Gary Arthur Thomson

iUniverse, Inc.
Bloomington

Ring Papa Ring!
The Story of An American Family

Copyright © 2013 by Gary Arthur Thomson

All rights reserved. No part of this book may be used or reproduced by any means, graphic, electronic, or mechanical, including photocopying, recording, taping or by any information storage retrieval system without the written permission of the publisher except in the case of brief quotations embodied in critical articles and reviews.

iUniverse books may be ordered through booksellers or by contacting:

iUniverse
1663 Liberty Drive
Bloomington, IN 47403
www.iuniverse.com
1-800-Authors (1-800-288-4677)

Because of the dynamic nature of the Internet, any web addresses or links contained in this book may have changed since publication and may no longer be valid. The views expressed in this work are solely those of the author and do not necessarily reflect the views of the publisher, and the publisher hereby disclaims any responsibility for them.

Any people depicted in stock imagery provided by Thinkstock are models, and such images are being used for illustrative purposes only.

Certain stock imagery © Thinkstock.

ISBN: 978-1-4759-8737-9 (sc)
ISBN: 978-1-4759-8738-6 (hc)
ISBN: 978-1-4759-8739-3 (e)

Printed in the United States of America

iUniverse rev. date: 05/07/2013

The authors wish to gratefully acknowledge and thank
the Fredrick Way Jr. Collection
for permission to use the pictures of the Klinefelter Steamboats
and to
Dean Luff
for graciously allowing us to use the picture
of his Native Arrowhead Collection
from the site of the Paisley Ranch

Family Tradition ± History

"History is the enemy of memory. The two stalk each other across the fields of the past, claiming the same terrain." [1]

—Richard White

"Happy Fourth of July. Well, scratch that. We mean: Happy Second of July." [2]

—Denise Kurnan & Joseph D'Agnesi

This book tells the story of one American family. Several family trees came together in two people, Blanche Klinefelter and Herbert Thomson—our grandparents. As writers, we are two grandsons who have corroborated to tell this story. Like weaving a tapestry, we have tried to interpret the story of our particular family in the context of unfolding European and American history.

This is a book about our family and its stories. We write about eras long, long ago as well as times closer to the present day. As two cousins, we have two points-of-view about these times and places. As the French would have it, *"Vive la différence."* Our diversity makes us stronger! Our corroboration sparks a certain energy and vitality. By e-mail we are often back and forth several times a

---

[1] Richard White, *Remembering Ahanagran*. NY: Hill and Wang, 1998, p. 4.

[2] Denise Kurnan and Joseph D'Agnesi, *Signing Their Lives Away*. Philadelphia: Quirk Press, 2009, p. 10.

day to sort out a situation a few generations earlier. We have five documented steamboat captains in our family. We have the military records of soldiers in the American Revolutionary War and the American Civil War. We have accumulated many bits and pieces of information—marriage certificates, homestead registrations, ships' logs, church records, minutes of the Continental Congress, warrants for arrest, bookkeeping of purchases, platted territories and towns, labeled pictures, and inscribed cemetery stones. Many personal letters recall family anecdotes and incidents. People like Aunt May remember how it was. We owe an immense debt to our family now in the heavenly places who graciously helped us to understand things the way they were. Their stories are the seeds for everything this book tries to convey.

It is easy to confuse family traditions with history. *"History is the enemy of memory. The two stalk each other across the fields of the past, claiming the same terrain."* Remembered family stories trail off into forgotten places. Each in his own way, we are historians. We have benefited from each other's approaches. Historians follow cautiously checking records. Memory can be misleading. But stories always have some basis in the past. The heart of our book is where the recollected stories and history meet.

Dean Ackermann Thomson
Gary Arthur Thomson

Contents

Grave of William Hurrie in Old Pine Churchyard in Philadelphia

William signed his name Hurrie which is the ordinary Scottish spelling. The signature of William Hurrie appears in the *Papers of the Continental Congress* compiled 1774-1789: Record Group 360 in a letter dated 20 September 1779. The DAR inadvertently misspelled his name on the bronze plaque.

The Pennsylvania State House became Independence Hall

Ring Papa! Ring!

The waiting boy saw the door thrown open and John Hancock waved him the high sign. Without a word, Arthur raced up the three flights of belfry stairs to where his father, William Hurrie, stood poised and waiting beneath the heavy, cracked bell.

"Ring Papa! Ring!" the lad shouted, and William Hurrie gave the big bell voice to fill Philadelphia with the sound of freedom. A Declaration of Independence had been composed and signed by 55 brave citizens. They signed with fear and trembling because they knew they were committing treason. Treason against King Georg III. But they knew they were creating something new. A new nation—America.

1

4 July 1776! That was the date. The date the boy told his father, "Ring Papa! Ring!"

William Hurrie who rang the Liberty Bell was our ancestor. He was in charge of Independence Hall. When the British vandalized the Hall, William Hurrie restored it. He was our ancestor!

Nearing his hundredth birthday, J. S. Klinefelter stood erect and patrician as he retold the story that gave his family an American authenticity. His oldest daughter, Blanche sat respectfully and proud as she listened to the telling for the umpteenth time. Five generations of his family were gathered and the youngest generation took in the story with wide eyes as if the event had happened only yesterday!

We all called him Grandpa Klinefelter. Most everyone in the community called him Grandpa Klinefelter. On his hundredth birthday, Grandpa Klinefelter was reciting our family's *oral tradition*.

The Liberty Bell

The fact is William Hurrie rang the bell on 8 July 1776! [3] William Hurrie was the sexton and official bell ringer of the Pennsylvania Statehouse in Philadelphia, afterwards called Independence Hall. Ronn Schaeffer, historian of Old Pine Street Church, sets the record straight:

> *"William Hurrie became an international " folk-hero" when he rang the Statehouse Bell 100 times to call people for the first public reading of the Declaration of Independence on July 8*[th]*, 1776.*
>
> *"Records indicate that Hurrie was paid a large sum of money to clean up the mess at the Statehouse when the British abandoned Philadelphia. His bill for work between June 26*[th]*—August 17*[th]*, 1778 included: paint, lumber, plaster, . . . and several quarts of whiskey . . . apparently used as an incentive to hasten the job.*
>
> *"The Declaration of Independence was formally read on July 8*[th] *in the presence of many spectators."* [4]

"Old Pine" Street Church is the only pre-Revolutionary Presbyterian structure still standing in Philadelphia. "Old Pine" was built in 1768 as a chapel of the "Old Buttonwood" Presbyterian congregation of 1704. "Old Pine" is a Greek-revival edifice with Corinthian columns and giant doors. Although Philadelphia is

---

3 Ronn Schaeffer, *Notes on William Hurrie*, historian of Old Pine Presbyterian Church in Philadelphia.

Denise Kiernan & Joseph D'Agnese, *Signing Their Lives Away* (Philadelphia: Quirk Books, 2009, p. 10 ff.)

4 Ronn Schaeffer, *Notes on William Hurrie*, historian of Old Pine Presbyterian Church in Philadelphia.

associated with William Penn and the Quaker faith, in fact by
1739, Presbyterians outnumbered all other religious denominations
in Philadelphia.[5] *"When Cornwallis was driven back to ultimate
retreat and surrender at Yorktown, all of the colonels of the Colonial
Army but one were Presbyterian elders. More than one-half of all
the soldiers and officers of the American Army during the Revolution
were Presbyterians."* [6]

In 1771 George Duffield (1732-1790) was voted to be the
minister of Old Pine Street Church. Some dissenters failed to lock
him out. The national issue of independence from England was on
the horizon. Duffield preached for American Independence. On
17 May 1776 John Adams wrote to his wife, Abigail, that Duffield
had preached a sermon which likened King Georg III's treatment
of Americans as being akin to Pharaoh's treatment of the Israelites.
John Adams found George Duffield to be *"a man of genius and
eloquence."* After another sermon, Adams wrote to his wife that
Duffield *"filled and swelled the bosom of every hearer."* George
Washington sought out Duffield as an advisor. At this same time
in Virginia, Patrick Henry was making the urgent appeal *"Give
me liberty, or give me death."* [7]

From the pulpit of Old Pine, George Duffield enlisted soldiers;
sixty men from his congregation followed him into the army,
many serving with distinction. Among the sixty who signed up

---

5 "Old Pine Street Presbyterian Church," Independence Hall Association in
Philadelphia. (USHistory.org)

6 J. R. Sizoo, *They Seek a Country: The American Presbyterians*, edited by
Galus Jackson Slosser, editor. New York: Macmillan, 1955, p. 155.

7 Denise Kiernan & Joseph D'Agnese, *Signing Their Lives Away: The Fame
and Misfortune of the Men who Signed The Declaration of Independence.*
Philadelphia: Quirk Books, 2009.

were William Hurrie and his son, Arthur Hurrie, and his son-in-law, Captain John McGinley.

Duffield's oratory did not go unnoticed by the British forces in Philadelphia. He was so inimical; they put a price on his head. Old Pine was trashed whilst the Church of England next door was left unscathed. British soldiers chopped up the pews for firewood. They turned the shell of Old Pine into a makeshift hospital for their wounded. Later the abrasive British cobbled Old Pine into a stopgap stable for their animals.

In the meantime Duffield was rallying colonial soldiers in support of liberty from tyranny. He was chaplain of the Pennsylvania Militia. When the war was over, Duffield got busy restoring the Old Pine congregation and building. On 1 October 1777, the Chaplain of the Continental Congress deserted their cause and went over to the British side. Congress appointed Duffield "who was not a traitor." Duffield remained the minister of Old Pine Church until his death on 2 February 1790.

The sixty men from Old Pine who followed Duffield into the American Revolutionary War acquitted themselves with honor. John Steele was field officer the day Cornwallis surrendered at Yorktown in 1781. William Linnard artificed cannon fire at Germantown. The Brits offered a reward for George Latimer—dead or alive. Our ancestor, William Hurrie and his son, Arthur, were foot soldiers.

In 1777, the capital of the United States was Philadelphia, Pennsylvania. The British Navy bombarded Fort Island Battery[8]

---

8 Fort Island Battery Fort was also called Mud Island Fort, Deep Water Island Fort and later, Fort Mifflin.

situated just below Philadelphia. This fort blocked the British until General Washington moved his army to Valley Forge. Washington put Captain John McGinley in charge of the fort with a garrison of 165 men. John McGinley was also our ancestor.

John McGinley married Margaret Hurrie, daughter of William Hurrie. Their daughter, Ann McGinley married Christian Stetler of Trappe, Pennsylvania. Ann and Christian Stetler are buried in the Augustus Lutheran Cemetery at Trappe. Their son was Abner Stetler.

Abner Stetler and his wife Caroline Garrison made that long journey from Philadelphia to Pittsburgh with two small sons in one of the old Conestoga Wagons to start a new life. Abner Stetler was a boilermaker in Pittsburgh—*Abner Stetler and Sons.* Perhaps Abner could have made some of the boilers for the many Klinefelter Steamboats in that era. Mark Twain yarns the story of the *SS Pennsylvania* that had four boilers explode when Captain John Klinefelter was getting shaved!

Abner and Caroline named their daughter Caroline. Moving from one generation to another, Caroline Stetler was the grandmother who raised Blanche, our grandmother.

Caroline's brother, William, gave his life in the Battle of Slaughter Mountain in the Civil War on 9 August 1862. In Culpepper County, Virginia, General Stonewall Jackson led his Confederate Army in a counterattack that slaughtered the Union Army that day. William was buried in a mass grave.

A month later, the Union Army won a Pyrrhic victory at The Battle on The Bridge over Antietam Creek; 17 September 1862 recalls the bloodiest day in the history of American warfare.

Emotions were running high and President Abraham Lincoln proclaimed the emancipation of all slaves. Caroline's suitor, Joseph Klinefelter, was wounded at Antietam Creek. When he returned to convalesce at Pittsburgh, Caroline and Joseph were married on 26 November 1862. In January, Joseph returned to artifice the cannons on the battlefield.

Joseph had two brothers who fought in the Civil War—Judge fought at Antietam and George Jesse enlisted at age fourteen!

William Hurrie was born in Scotland. He died in 1781 at the time Cornwallis surrendered at Yorktown marking the final British defeat and the triumph of the American Revolution.[9]

In 1886 a great grandson of William Hurrie wrote *A Poor Orphan Boy*. In it are these words regarding William Hurrie:

Just before the war was ended, he was taken sick with Bilious fever and when the news arrived that Cornwallis was taken, they tried to keep it from him fearing the excitement would cause his death, but hearing the night watchman repeat it, he enquired its meaning and they had to tell him.

Soon after, his son came and said, "Good news to thee my father!"

Said he, "Good news to thee my son, my Joy is in Heaven!"

That night he died!

---

9 Jim Webb, *Born Fighting: How The Scots-Irish Shaped America*. New York: Broadway Books, 2004, p. 133.

William Hurrie & Mary
|
   Margaret Hurrie & John McGinley
    |
      Ann McGinley & Christian Stetler
       |
         Abner Stetler & Caroline Garrison
          |
            Caroline Stetler & Joseph Klinefelter
             |
               Judge S. Klinefelter & Emma Ackermann
                |
                  Blanche Klinefelter & Herbert J. Thomson

Blanche Klinefelter

Paula, daughter of Alma Thomson Caddy, cares for this portrait of her grandmother, Blanche.

Herbert and Blanche Klinefelter Thomson

A Chance Meeting

It was a chance meeting. Once upon a time a fashionable eastern girl and an enterprising boy from the west met on a train, fell in love, and began a dynasty. It happened like this.

40 years after the last gun was fired in the American Civil War, veteran Joseph Klinefelter arranged to attend the National GAR Encampment on September 7-8, 1905 in Denver. During the war, he was an artificer firing the cannons. At The Battle on The Bridge over Antietam Creek, Joseph was wounded and captured by the Confederates. Eleven days later he was moved to Libby Prison, and then paroled eight days after that. He recovered to march with General Sherman to Atlanta.

Now, four decades later, Joseph was 63; the Denver gathering of Union soldiers would be significant for him. Veterans found solace in their battle-forged bonds; they remembered their fallen comrades. At "Blue and Gray" reunions, veterans of both sides made conciliatory overtures and celebrated their collective American identity.

The powerful steam locomotive puffed out of Pittsburgh and headed west. His wife, Caroline, and their 18 years old granddaughter, Blanche, accompanied Joseph. They rode in a First Class compartment; Joseph and Caroline sat facing their pretty granddaughter. Through their window, they watched Ohio passing by. Their car may have been a Pullman that converted into beds at night; the journey from Pittsburgh to Denver totaled 1500 miles!

The train stopped at Oberlin near Cleveland where Blanche's father, J.S. Klinefelter was now living with his second wife, Lois, and two daughters, Caroline and Hortense; later the half-sister's would marry professors; Caroline would remain at Oberlin College with her botanist husband and Hortense would move to Hartford, Connecticut.

Blanche's mother, Emma Ackerman Klinefelter, had died in childbirth when she was only 25. Her grandparents, Caroline and Joseph Klinefelter, raised Blanche.

America had a super public transportation system in 1905. That year represented the acme of locomotive development of the Pennsylvania Railroad. Fueled with 13 tons of coal and 5600 gallons of water, the 4-4-0 steamer pulled the Pennsylvania Special on a ten-hour schedule between Pittsburgh and Chicago with an excellent on-time record.

Thinking back, Joseph Klinefelter was born in 1842. That year, the first covered wagons began to move west across the plains on the Oregon Trail.

Two decades later in 1862, Joseph was called to arms in the Civil War. That year, President Abraham Lincoln signed the Pacific Railroad Act; but by the end of the war the Union Pacific had yet to spike a rail.

Speaking of pounding railroad spikes, the USA standard gauge is 4 feet, 8.5 inches between the rails. That's because English expatriates designed American railroads.

Why 4 feet, 8.5 inches? Because back in England those who built railroad cars used the same jigs that they had used to build wagons.

So, why did English wagons have 4 feet, 8.5 inches wheel spacing? That is the spacing of the wheel ruts on the old Roman Roads in England. Roman chariots grooved ruts that later wagons had to match to avoid destroying their wagon wheels. And so it goes!

By the summer of 1870, the Burlington Railway (CB&Q) reached Lincoln—the newly designated capital of Nebraska. By 1882, the rails connected Chicago all the way to Denver. By 1905, the Burlington Railway had 12,000 route miles in 14 states. America had a public transportation system second to none. Every village and hamlet had a railroad station, a livery stable, a hotel, restaurants, and often an opera house!

In 1905 Joseph Klinefelter was taking his wife and granddaughter to Denver. The GAR—The Grand Army of The Republic—was meeting in beautiful Colorado Springs. They were on the train to Denver, Colorado. Joseph and Caroline

Klinefelter with their pretty granddaughter, Blanche. A branch line connected the cities.

During the summer of 1905, a young man named Herbert Thomson, our grandfather, traveled the rails all the way to Oregon to visit his Aunt Mary and his cousins, Herbert James Thorne and Georgia Graham.

In September of 1905, Herbert was returning by train from Oregon. From his window seat, he craned his head this way and that to watch the snaking train meandering through the mountains. Sometime he could look ahead and see the locomotive starting to cross a high wooden trestle that he knew his own railroad car would soon cross. Looking far down into the canyon gave him the shivers.

Sometimes it seemed they were in a deep valley even deeper than the cascading river beside the train track. Then they were clinging to a slim ledge cut into the solid rock hundreds of feet above the valley floor. The railroad journey from Oregon to Colorado passed through the scenery of the Utah Salt Flats, the Idaho potato fields, the Snake River with its jumping salmon, and the volcanic wonderland near Yellowstone. It was amazing how the railroad had networked the west since Abe Lincoln signed the act back in 1862. Herb dozed to the rhythmic clickity-clack of the riveted rails as they moved through the eerie moonlight in the mountains. He dreamt of a bobcat that he had encountered while milking late at night back at the family homestead in Nebraska.

Americans have certain National Monuments that everybody knows about—like Pike's Peak. Americans tell about their Uncle Somebody who breezed up the steep switchback ascent in his Buick Touring Car, whilst Uncle Johnny kerplunk, kerplunk, kerplunked along with his Model T Ford. Uncle Johnny pressed his planetary gear peddle for every little rise in the road. That of course was in the Roaring Twenties when there were automobiles; in 1905 only a railroad had made its serpentine way up Pike's Peak to where the GAR veterans encamped at the summit.

Years later, our dads and uncles—Alexander, Arthur, Alfred, George and Reid, the five sons of Blanche and Herbert—would reminisce about their summer adventures in the Rockies of Colorado and Wyoming. They especially remembered Yellowstone Park. They recalled the night when they were sleeping in their tent. Suddenly there was the rattle and clang of kettles, pots and pans. A bear was in their cooking larder. In the consternation, the tent collapsed. The bear got his nose caught in a can of honey and departed dragging a sheet! A further embellishment to the story recalled that Old Faithful Geyser belched and spewed just as the bear was making his exit.

40th Anniversary of Civil War Veterans Medallion of Pike's Peak in 1905

The long platform of the station in Colorado Springs was full of veterans. Probably Blanche and her Grandmother Caroline remained in lovely Colorado Springs in one of the fine hotels. Joseph and his fellow Civil War vets assaulted the steep grade to Pike's Peak—another thirty mountain miles! The Peak would be the perfect setting for the Medallion Ceremony celebrating forty years since the Civil War ended.

Joseph Klinefelter had fought in the Civil War, the war in the United States between the Union and the Confederacy. This Civil War lasted from 1861 until 1865.

Joseph with fellow veterans sought out occasions to gather together, to relive their shared experiences, to find solace in their battle-forged bonds, to celebrate their heroic deeds, and to commemorate the sacrifices of their fallen comrades.

This symbolic reunion took place on 7-8 September 1905. Today, their silent parade was on a mountain peak. Tomorrow, they would be returning home.

 His Move   1905 Gibson Girl

The American young woman of 1905, the Gibson Girl, was idealized in sketches by the illustrator Charles Dana Gibson with a clothing style marked by a high neck, puffed sleeves, and a tightly fitted waistline.

A Chance Meeting took place on the railroad platform. Joseph jostled the luggage. From the look of things, Blanche and her Grandmother Caroline had made some purchases in the boutiques and shops of Colorado Springs. It was the era of the Gibson Girl and appropriate hatboxes surmounted the suitcases.

A well-dressed, dapper young man stood nearby on the railroad platform. He was about to board the train. He carried a simple suitcase.

Then the young man made a move to help Joseph with his mountain of luggage. The older man certainly accepted the help with appreciation. Soon they had the luggage stowed away in their compartment on the train.

"Would you like to join us?" Joseph inquired of the helpful young man. "You could sit by my granddaughter in our compartment. There is ample space for four people."

And that is how pretty Blanche Klinefelter and dapper Herbert Thomson met.

Five hundred miles of animated conversation ensued as they crossed the Great Plains of western Colorado and the Platte Valley of Nebraska. At Lincoln, Nebraska, Herbert got off the train, reluctantly waving goodbye to Blanche and her grandparents. That was in September of 1905.

For three months, they wrote their *billet-doux*—their love letters.

In December of 1905, Blanche and Herbert were married! At the Shady Avenue Baptist Church in Pittsburgh, Pennsylvania with Edwin M. Stanton officiating, Blanche Mabel Klinefelter and Herbert James Thomson were wed at 7:15 on 6 December 1905.

The Prophet House just south of the Palmyra High School was their first home in Nebraska. Then they began a series of moves until they built a new house in 1910. At a small house on the periphery of Palmyra, their first son, Alexander, was born in 1907. On the Mortimer Farm East of Palmyra, Arthur was born on 19 August 1908. Herb purchased an 80-acre farm and 160-acre farm. Alfred was born in the new house in 1910. Joseph & Caroline Klinefelter came from Pittsburgh to visit in September 1910.

In 1913 Herb and Blanche bought the first electrically lit Buick Touring Car from the Sidles' dealership in Lincoln, Nebraska.

1913 Buick Touring Car with Electric Lights

World War I was fought from 1914 to 1918. Having been born on the 17th of December 1875, Herbert was 42 when the war broke out. When the draft was instituted in September 1918, Herbert registered—#1074. But the war was soon over.

The Family of Blanche and Herbert Thomson in 1915

The Canadian sequence in the lives of Herbert and Blanche began on 24 August 1914 when Herbert traded 80 Nebraska acres and $5000 for a half-section of land in Halkirk in the Province of Alberta. He made the deal sight unseen with a man named John Judkins. Herbert was issued title to the Halkirk Farm on 10 October 1914. Later he purchased a second half-section, 320 acres, at Stettler, Alberta. Border crossing documents indicate that Herbert crossed into Canada at North Portal, Saskatchewan with money specifically for buying the Stettler Farm in Alberta. The two parcels of land were 35 miles apart.

But Blanche and Herbert continued to live in Palmyra.

In 1920 Herbert and Blanche moved their family to Canada. They crossed the border at North Portal on 4 March 1920 on their way to the Province of Alberta. They settled at the Stettler Farm before the land title was actually issued.

Farmstead of Herbert and Blanche Thomson at Stettler, Alberta, CANADA
George, Reid, lady, Blanche, Faith, and Alfred

May Viola Thomson was born 12 July 1920 at the Stettler Farm house with the help of Grandma Marshall, a neighborly midwife. Herbert received title to the Stettler farm in December 1920. Their school age children attended the Bignell country school.

Bignell Country School — Lonely 35 mile road from Stettler to Halkirk

One year later in October of 1921, Herb sold the farm to his brother, John Thomson. Herb and Blanche moved their family back to Nebraska. Was it *wanderlust*?

Seven years later, Herb bought the Canadian farm back from brother John. In March 1928, their sons, Alexander and Arthur, boarded two railroad cars in Palmyra; a flat car held a new John Deere Model D Tractor and other farm equipment, and a boxcar contained livestock. The two young men lived in the boxcar. With the door slid open, they watched the countryside go by. Their route took them to Minneapolis, Minnesota before veering northwest to Winnipeg, Manitoba. The law in the United States permitted two persons to accompany the two railroad cars. Indeed, it was encouraged. In Canada, however, only one person was allowed. A Royal Canadian Mounted Policeman removed Arthur from the train. Arthur was going to walk beside the Mountie but the policeman rudely insisted that he walk in front of him.

In Stettler, Alberta, Alexander and Arthur unloaded the railroad cars. At the Stettler Farm and the Halkirk Farm, they tilled the soil and planted spring wheat. They cared for all of the family livestock.

In late summer, Blanche and Herbert arrived with the rest of their family in time for the harvest. Herb took his sons to Big Valley, south of Stettler where they all enjoyed a rodeo. Every Sunday, the family attended the Stettler Baptist Church.

Alfred drove a team of horses on a grain binder from the Stettler Farm to the Halkirk Farm. The distance was 35 miles of long, lonely stretches of country roads. He wasn't sure where he was. He thought he was lost. About that time, the family caught up to him in the car. He felt better then!

The Granaries on the Halkirk Farm being 35 miles from the Stettler home place, Herbert and his sons slept in these granaries during the harvest. There was no house. The John Deere Model D pulled a three-bottom plow.

Eventually they returned to Nebraska again and to farming at Palmyra. But they continued to visit and oversee their farms in Canada. Dean Ackermann Thomson retains the Stettler farmstead to this day.

The following is a roster of the children of Blanche and Herbert with their spouses:

Alexander Joseph Thomson 4 March 1907—19 August 1964 wed
Donna Isabelle Van Allen 10 August 1932
Arthur Klinefelter Thomson 19 August 1908—31 January 1998
wed Verna Lorraine Wall 14 December 1932
Alfred Ackermann Thomson 31 March 1910—July 30 2008
married Helen Esther Caddy October 21 1936
George Ronald Thomson 22 April 1913—5 May 1990 married
Viola Faye Lanning 6 November 1935
Reid James Thomson 26 January 1915—2 December 1964
married Dorothy Baldwin 10 July 1944
Faith Mabel Thomson 13 Dec 1916 —18 Sept 2002 married
Lloyd Clair Nash 25 August 1937
May Viola Thomson 12 July 1920—still living, married Dale
Pershing Lamb 9 October 1940
Alma Elberta Thomson 22 May 1922 —2011 married William
Joshua Eugene Caddy 24 August 1944

Herbert James Thomson died on the 8th of March 1948. We
had a big snow at that time and the snowplow came through
so that we could get to his funeral. He was born 17 December
1875.

Blanche Klinefelter Thomson died on the 21st of June 1964.
She was born 27 September 1887.

Blanche's father, J. S. Klinefelter died two months later.
Having been born on 22 July 1864, Grandpa Klinefelter lived to
be a centenarian dying on 9 August 1964.

Blanche

Signposted as a Nature Park, *The Spessart* is a forested mountainous region of Hesse-Darmstadt in central Germany. Florsbach is in the heart of The Spessart. The Main River makes a 300-mile horseshoe around three sides of The Spessart. About 50 miles to the west, the Main River joins the Rhine River at Mainz. The river journey from Mainz to Rotterdam is approximately 350 miles.

The Florsbach Church in The Spessart; the photo was taken in the cemetery above the church. Klinefelter's and Kunkel's worshiped here; they were baptized, marrled, and burled here.

A Conversation in Spessart Forest

"In war when people are at each others' mercies, all pretense crumbles."

—Harold Pinter

After chopping a deep cut into the base, and before the great oak fell, Hans Jorg Klinefelter lounged back with his hands on the knob of his axe handle. Looking through a clearing in the trees, his eyes adjusted to rest on some far peaks of *The Spessart*. Hans was a forester and these wooded mountains were his domains. The tree he was felling was a special fine-grain given the name

Spessart Oak. When his own Hessian prince[10] also inherited the kingship of England, English cabinetmakers came here seeking *Spessart Oak*.

When the sound of the axe fell silent, his son, Hans Peter, took the opportunity to talk.

"When our German princes became English kings, it seemed like an honor," he said.

"Yes," his father replied, "I watched the royal procession pass through Spessart Forest when our Elector became King Georg I of England."

"Exactly," said Hans Peter. "And now Georg II has come to the English throne.[11]"

His father nodded affirmatively.

"It is fine for these English to want our Spessart Oak," Hans Peter said. "But now these English, through their Hessian Prince, want us to be their soldiers to fight their battles for their empire."

"You're worried about being drafted?"

"For sure! I've got a wonderful wife, Eva, and a growing family.

With a slight blush, Hans Jorg admitted, "Her parents, Johannes and Anna Kunkel, have already visited Margaretha and I about it."

---

10 Prince Georg I was one of eight Electors of the royal Hapsburg family who elected the Holy Roman Emperor. German speaking, Georg I inherited the English throne through his mother Sophia who was granddaughter of King James I of England. This English dynasty of German origin has continued to the present day. In this book to distinguish these kings of German origin, we will spell their names as Georg I, Georg II and Georg III.

11 King Georg II was the English monarch from 1727-1760. A warrior king who led his troops in battle, he put down the Jacobite Rebellion and was victorious in the Seven Years War.

"So! You've already talked about this with the Kunkels?"
Hans Jorg nodded again.

Hans Jorg stepped back from his axe and looked directly into his son's eyes. "They are worried about their grandchildren," he said slowly. "Your mom and I are too."

Hans Peter was taken aback a bit. He was surprised to be caught unawares by his father. "So what else did they say?" he slowly inquired.

"They talked about where you might go."

"Now you tell me they are making our travel plans!" Hans Peter was slightly nettled.

Hans Jorg ignored his son's irritation and went on, "They talked about a place called Germantown[12] in America. They feel strongly that you and Eva should emigrate."

"You talk as if it's all settled!" Hans Peter grimaced. Then he said, "Actually I should be grateful. Eva and I thought the family would be upset if we took off and left you."

Hans Jorg made a move to use his axe again, but then he paused. "Yah!" he said, "In fact, we first talked together about it at your wedding at the Kempfenbrunn Kirke."[13]

---

12 First settled by German immigrants in 1683, Germantown is on northwestern periphery of Philadelphia in Pennsylvania.

13 The wedding of Hans Peter Klinefelter and Eva Elizabeth Kunkel, daughter of Johannes Sebastian Kunkel & Anna Samer, took place in the church at Kempfenbrunn on 16 June 1724 two miles from Florsbach. Lutheran church records began in the year 1711. Within the forested mountainous region of The Spessart, Florsbach and Kempfenbrunn are in a long beautiful valley, Florsbachthal.

"Our wedding was *before* Georg II became the English war hawk," barked Hans Peter. "Now he needs a multitude of soldiers. Eva and I and our little family can still emigrate. We've been talking about it incessantly all the time."

The sun had moved to The Spessart Forest skyline. The trees were silhouetted in the gathering twilight. The nocturnal birds and animals were beginning to make their presence felt in the deepening shadows of the gigantically tall trees of The Spessart.

Hans Jorg shifted the weight of his giant torso. He let the blade of his axe drop and set itself cockeyed in the sawn-off trunk.

"Actually," he recounted, "it was just before I was born. There was an English Quaker named Admiral William Penn. The king owed him a fortune that had not been repaid at the time of the Admiral's death. The younger William Penn had been imprisoned several times for his religious views. After being released from his last imprisonment, he approached the king about the debt owed his father. The king responded by giving him a large tract of land in America that Penn named Pennsylvania."

Hans Peter was listening attentively.

His father continued, "William Penn got out of that English jail and came here. He was recruiting people for his Quaker colony in America.[14] Lots of people went with him then. Now he has this Germantown just outside of Philadelphia."

---

14 William Penn's *Journal of his travels in Holland and Germany in 1677 in the service of the Gospel.* London: Darton and Harvey, Fourth edition 1835. He founded the Quaker colony of Pennsylvania in 1681.

"Do you have to become a Quaker to go there?" questioned his son.

"No. The Quakers aren't that way. They espouse religious tolerance."

"Eva and I are really serious about this."

"I know. Margaretha and I have prayed about it for a long time. We have even considered emigration ourselves to help you. How will you go?"

"That's a hard question."

"You can't go through France. King Louis XIV[15] revoked the Edict of Religious Toleration[16] in 1685 when I was a boy. He settled his religious wars by killing half his population. He slaughtered French Protestants by the thousands. There is a whole colony of Huguenot refugees at the Rhine Falls on the German border with France. Your German Protestant family cannot travel safely in France. Old Louis XIV has been carrying on for seventy years! He settled his religious wars by getting rid of half his people!"

"So we'll have to go down the Rhine to Holland," young Hans acquiesced.

"You will have to go down the Rhine!" his father affirmed and nodded his head again.

"But that's a big problem."

---

15 The reign of Louis XIV (1643-1715) was the longest in French history. Louis waged three major wars: the Dutch War (1672-1678), the War of the Grand Alliance (1688-1697), and the War of the Spanish Succession (1701-1714).

16 The Edict of Nantes, granting limited religious and civil liberties to the Huguenots (French Protestants), was issued in 1598 by Henry IV of France and revoked in 1685 by Louis XIV.

"What do you mean?"

"Every bloody German duke has a toll chain across the river. Thirty-six corrupt watchtowers patrolling the Rhine."

"We will need a fat wallet."

"They'll stop you and take their own sweet time wheedling your money."

"I've heard that it takes longer to go down the Rhine to Rotterdam, than it takes to cross the Atlantic Ocean to America!"

"And more money! They're in cahoots with King Georg II. He gets his cut."

The forested Spessart peaks were silhouetted against the setting sun when father and son made their way down the valley to Florsbach.

Forested Mountains of *The Spessart*—Florsbachthal Valley

Klein is the German word for "small." *Felder* translates as "fields." In Florsbachtal, literally "in the valley of Florsbach," there were many "small fields." In Florsbach, they were the Kleinfelder's.

Hans Jorg Kleinfelder appears in the parish records of Florsbach where he was born about 1671—a forest ranger and game warden in Der Spessart. Hans Jorg was the son of Michael Kleinfelder II born in 1637 and grandson of Michael Kleinfelder I born about the Year 1600. Hans Jorg married Margaretha Rheinhardt.

When Hans Jorg and Margaretha's granddaughter, Katharina married Hans Peter Spessart in 1742, she still signed as Katharina Kleinfelder. Eight years later, with their infant son, Michael, they sailed for the New World. Somewhere lost in the mists of time, Kleinfelder changed to Klinefelter.

Eva's parents, Johannes and Anna Kunkel, spearheaded the venture of emigration to the New World; they made the arduous journey in 1748 on a ship named *Patience*. Johannes kept a log about their journey:

The river voyage took some four to six weeks because of frequent stops at customs houses along the way. There were thirty-six customs houses; at each the boats were examined when it suited the convenience of the officials.... The cost of the journey down the Rhine was generally 40 florins and the cost from Rotterdam to Philadelphia was 60 Florins with children 5 to 10 years paying half price and the younger being free.[17]

Young Kimberly Ann stood by the ship's railing looking out at the ocean waves. Beside her stood her mother, Jeanette Kroese Thomson holding her baby sister, Shannon Adele, three-months-old, and her father, Gary Arthur Thomson. They were returning from a year of post-graduate study in Edinburgh, Scotland. The

---

[17] Research of Walter Klinefelter: *The Log of Johannes Kunkel on The Ship Patience 1748.*

post World War II ship was named the *Media* belonging to the Cunard Lines. They moved to the side of the deck where they could observe the Statue of Liberty as they came into New York Harbor on Palm Sunday, 1961. They had been at sea for five days coming from Liverpool, England.

Youthful Jacob stood on the deck of a ship. Jacob was Kimberly's ancestor two centuries earlier. Jacob looked out at the ocean waves. Jacob stood between his mother Apollonia, and his father Johannes Michael Klinefelter by the rail. Jacob looked over his shoulder at his grandfather Hans Peter and his grandmother Eva. Grandpa Hans winked at Jacob. Three generations of Jacob's family were on the *Duke of Bedford* in 1751. He had lots of uncles and aunts.[18] Another aunt and uncle had come to America in 1749 on the ship *Priscilla*.

Too youthful to realize the implications and the sacrifice of his family, Jacob was aware that they were going to America! Everyone was excited, so he was also excited. America! He looked out at the ocean in wonder! He looked up at the white sails that billowed in the wind. "The wind moves our ship across the water," his father explained. "And the sails catch the wind," Jacob added. Then he pointed ahead and spoke again. "Winds to America!" Grandpa Hans clapped his hands and smiled. Then Hans pointed like his youthful grandson and reiterated the powerful word, "America." The word contained all their dreams and hopes. Jacob

---

18 In a memorandum of 6 September 1910, Joseph Klinefelter wrote, *"My Grandfather was born in Germany. I also remember my Grandmother on my Father's side. She died when I was about 4 or 5 years old."*

In another memorandum of 1 January 1971, Caroline Klinefelter Shelton wrote, *"My Grandfather Joseph Klinefelter's grandfather (Jacob) was born in Germany. I have a translation of his record in Germany."*

liked their enthusiasm. "America," he said it again evoking cheers from all his family.

In 1751 three children of the German family named Spessart were also aboard the ship— Anna Margaretha Spessart, Michael Spessart and Hans Peter Spessart. Hans Peter Spessart had married Katharina Klinefelter, daughter of Eva and Hans, in 1742. They had a son, Michael Spessart, who had been born in 1750; he was just an infant on arrival in America.[19]

Upon arriving at Philadelphia on Saturday the 14th day of September, Hans Peter Klinefelter and two of his sons, John and George went immediately to the courthouse in Philadelphia. Ship's list C states: *"The foreigners whose names are underwritten imported in the Duke of Bedford, Richard Jeffries, Master, from Rotterdam and last from Portsmouth, did this day take the unusual qualifications and subscribe them."* They were required to take the oath of allegiance to King Georg II. It was an ironic piece of procedure for these immigrants from the Duchy of Hanover whose Elector was Georg II, to whom they already owed allegiance.

Hans Peter Klinefelter was carrying 445 gulden to make the voyage and re-establish himself in Pennsylvania![20] Hans Peter and Eva Klinefelter went to live in Berks and York Counties of Pennsylvania amongst German settlers. Three of their sons served in the Revolutionary War—George, John and Michael.[21]

Youthful Jacob would grow up to marry Susan Miller. They would have six sons and one daughter. One of those sons was our

---

19 The list of passengers on the *Duke of Bedford* shows Hans Peter Spessart below the name of Johannes Kleinfelter, his brother-in-law.

20 Lloyd Faller, *The Kleinfelter Family of 1673.*

21 *Early families of York County, Pennsylvania, Volume I,* pages 69-73.

ancestor, Jesse. Jacob would become a keelboat man; a keelboat is a riverboat with a keel but without sails, used for carrying freight. Via the Susquehanna River, Jacob transported immigrants from Baltimore to the interior by keelboat. Jacob paved the way for five of his six sons to become steamboat captains.

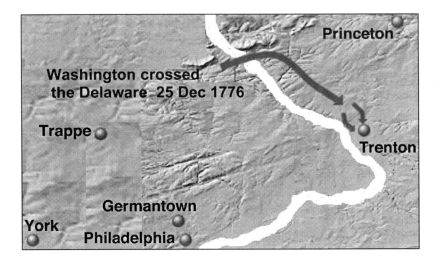

General Washington crossed the Delaware River and caught the British army unawares on Christmas Day 25 December 1776.

"Washington Crossing the Delaware," painted by Emanuel Leutze in 1851

Hessian Cousins Meet in 1776

Men are not prisoners of fate, but only prisoners of their own minds.

—Franklin D. Roosevelt

On Christmas Day 1776, General George Washington famously crossed the icy Delaware River and caught the British army off guard. In the altercation at Trenton that followed, General Washington captured a large detachment of soldiers including Henry, Michael and David Kunkel.

Recruited as they were from The Spessart countryside, the Kunkel brothers were torn by the tenuous relationship between King Georg III of Hanover and Prince Frederick II of Hesse. The disputing sovereigns arbitrarily grabbed vulnerable youth from the German countryside to fight their English and Prussian wars. The flimsy treaty between Georg III and Frederick II put youth in an equivocal situation. The duplicitous Frederick told Georg III that no Hessian *"shall be permitted to establish himself in America, without the consent of his sovereign."* But wily Georg III was quite happy to put coins in his own coffer by selling unfortunate dissidents as indentured servants.

When Henry, Michael and David Kunkel arrived they soon discovered that they were going to be forced to fight youth of their own Hessian homeland. It was difficult for them to protest or refuse.

On Christmas Eve 1776 the Kunkels were part of the unsuspecting British military encampment at Trenton, New Jersey. After all, it was Christmas Eve!

But that night, General Washington and his brave soldiers boldly turned the war around!

The next day a large number of captured soldiers including Henry, Michael and David Kunkel were wondering about their future. They were prisoners of war. POW's.

Michael Klinefelter was in the Colonial Army of General George Washington. He served with Captain Aquila Wiley in the 2nd Company, 5th Battalion, of the York County Militia. His rank was Private. In the resolution of this conflict, Michael Klinefelter had the opportunity to purchase Henry Kunkel as an indentured servant. [22] Speaking fluently in German, Michael Klinefelter and Henry Kunkel soon discovered that they were 4th generation

---

[22] Michael Kunkel was sold to a man in Pennsylvania. David Kunkel was sold to a man in Virginia.

descendants of Hans and Elizabeth Ickus Kunkel of Florsbach, Germany!

The bailout price would take seven years to pay off. Johannes Michael Klinefelter, a farmer who owned land, was already weighed down insufferable taxes on land. A Kunkel family historical document gives this record:

Mr. Kleinfelter bought Henry Kunkel (as an indentured servant). *Kleinfelter went for days trying to borrow money to pay the heavy tax, but was unable to do it. So he thought he would lose the land. Henry Kunkel asked him how much it would take. He opened his vest; around him he had a money belt in which was enough money to pay the tax. Kleinfelter deeded half of the land to Henry Kunkel, who in turn married Kleinfelter's daughter, Elizabeth Christina.*

* * * * *

The Yorkshire Dales in northern England are the picturesque countryside of James Herriot's *All Creatures Great and Small,* the PBS Television Series. The Dales are also the locale of the Bronte sisters—Charlotte, Emily and Anne, the novelists. The burned out manor house in Wycoller provided the setting of *Jane Eyre* by Charlotte Bronte in 1847. The moors at Hawick are the *Wuthering Heights* that Emily Bronte described in 1849. The Yorkshire Dales inspired the geography of *The Hobbit* (1937) and *The Lord of the Rings* (1954) by J. R. Tolkien who lived at Clitheroe.

William Penn sought to enroll Yorkshire Quakers in 1682 in a venture in the New World and thereby remove them from religious persecution in England. Non-conformist religious groups—Quakers, Presbyterians, Methodists, Baptists—were harassed and persecuted by the Crown and the Church of England. The Dissolution of The Monasteries by King Henry VIII destroyed monastic culture in England. Queen Elizabeth I sought to eradicate Roman Catholic families. The only alternative was to attend the Church of England.[23] The Non-conformists were left out in the cold!

Gary Arthur Thomson was minister of The United Reformed Church in Morpeth, England. Nearby was an ancient non-conformist church structure that was built on a county line. This line went down the center aisle of the sanctuary. In the 1600s, sheriffs acting in behalf of the Crown would harass non-conformist congregations. When the sheriff of one county would arrive on a Sunday morning, the congregation would promptly move across the aisle. Later, during the service, the sheriff of the other county might arrive so the worshippers would quickly move across the aisle into the opposite county. And so it went!

Giggleswick and Stackhouse are adjoining quaintly attractive villages in the Yorkshire Dales. In the 1600s Saint Akelda Church of England was well established in Giggleswick. According to tradition, Akelda had been an Anglo-Saxon princess raped by Vikings. Enforced by the sheriff, the official Church of Saint Akelda literally drove out non-conformists. The level of persecution was such that Quakers were willing to leave their beautiful Yorkshire Dales. When William Penn offered an alternative in 1682, these peaceful people were ready to seek a more tolerant place to live.

---

23 It is ironic that even in Ireland the two cathedrals in Dublin are Church of England dating to the troubled 1600s.. Even in Armagh, the cathedral seat of Saint Patrick is Church of England. Is it any wonder the Catholics are tweaked?

In 1682, a Quaker family named Stackhouse emigrated from Giggleswick and Stackhouse—their namesake village—to go on two ships commissioned by William Penn to the New World. The *HMS Lamb* transported the Stackhouse family and the *HMS Welcome* carried William Penn himself. After an arduous ocean journey in which many died of smallpox, the ships sailed up the Delaware River to make land in Pennsylvania on 27 October 1682.

Armed with a charter granted by England's King Charles II, William Penn (1644-1718) and one hundred travel-weary Quakers arrived in the New World aboard the <u>Welcome</u> on October 27, 1682, with the intention of establishing the founder's "holy experiment," a colony that would be free of the religious persecution they suffered abroad. Once safely docked in the Delaware Bay at New Castle, Penn traveled inland.[24]

Five generations later in the Stackhouse home at Tullytown, Pennsylvania on February 1822, Elizabeth Mason Stackhouse[25] married Joshua Brooks, a blacksmith by trade. James P. Scott, Justice of The Peace, performed the ceremony. They had six children; their daughter Anne Brooks married Jesse Klinefelter, a riverboat pilot.

Elizabeth Mason Stackhouse and Joshua Brooks were our great great great great grandparents. And to add another "great," Elizabeth's father's name was Stephen Stackhouse.

---

24   Rae Tyson, "Our First Friends, The Early Quakers," *Pennsylvania Heritage Magazine*, Volume XXXVII, Number 2 - Spring 2011.

25   This information comes from a family memoir to Elizabeth Mason Stackhouse. She was born on 19 March 1802 in Philadelphia, Pennsylvania. She was married at Tullytown, Pennsylvania 26 miles northeast of Philadelphia on the Delaware River. She died on 5 September 1901 in Pittsburgh. She was 99 years of age. Her father's name was Stephen Stackhouse.

Pittsburgh was the Industrial Capital of America in 1850

Pittsburgh is a city in Southwest Pennsylvania where the Allegheny and Monongahela Rivers form the Ohio River. In 1750 the French built Fort Duquesne here; the British took the fort in 1758 and renamed it Fort Pitt. During the age of industrialization, Pittsburgh played a major role in the shaping of America through steel, coal mining, inventions, technology and famous philanthropists.[26]

Five Klinefelter brothers were steamboat captains out of Pittsburgh— Michael, Thomas, Jesse, Jacob and John,

---

26 Dan Snow, *Death or Victory: The Battle For Québec and The Birth of Empire.* London: Harper Press, 2009. 1759 was the decisive year that set the stage for the American Revolution. 1759 was the year of the demise of New France and the accession of the British over North America. The years between 1759 and 1776 told the tales that precipitated the revolution in Philadelphia.

SS Messenger Steamboat

SS Hibernia II Steamboat

Captain Jesse Klinefelter skippered the *SS Hibernia II Steamboat* between Pittsburgh and Nashville. Among famous passengers who came aboard the steamboats of the Klinefelter brothers were Charles Dickens, Jenny Lind, and P T Barnum.

'S-t-e-a-m-boat a-comin'!'

"On the Mississippi, steamboat round the bend,
chug chug, chug chug, to the journey's end."
—American Folk Song

The river arched around a wide bend that the steamboat maneuvered with some difficulty. The heavy foliage of willows hung out from the shore and screened the view ahead. Negotiating the yawning turn, the palatial steamboat puffed into full view of the river town. Mark Twain described it dramatically:

*Presently a film of dark smoke appears above one of those remote 'points;' instantly a negro drayman, famous for his quick eye and prodigious voice, lifts up the cry, **'S-t-e-a-m-boat a-comin'!'** . . . Drays, carts, men, boys, all go hurrying from many quarters to a common center, the wharf. Assembled there, the people fasten their eyes upon the coming boat as upon a wonder they are seeing for the first time. And the boat IS rather a handsome sight, too. She is long and sharp and trim and pretty; she has two tall, fancy-topped chimneys, with a gilded device of some kind swung between them; a fanciful pilot-house, a glass and 'gingerbread', perched on top of the 'texas' deck behind them; the paddle-boxes are gorgeous with a picture or with gilded rays above the boat's name; . . . the upper decks are black with passengers; the captain stands by the big bell, calm, imposing, the envy of all; great volumes of the blackest smoke are rolling and tumbling out of the chimneys. . . the captain lifts his hand, a bell rings, the wheels stop; then they turn back, churning the water to foam, and the steamer is at rest.*[27]

Approximately 300 passengers experienced the cruise north from Nashville in the spring of 1851 on the *SS Messenger II.* Among the celebrities on board, P. T. Barnum stood out as America's Number One Showman. Barnum and Bailey had made the circus a favorite attraction that ordinary folk anticipated. Jenny Lind, his dazzling super star, moved amongst the doting, well-healed passengers. Elaborate staterooms and well-fitted cabins insured the comfort of the passengers.

Social climbers like Hattie MacDuncan and her obedient husband Archibald paid dearly from their frugal savings for this

[27] Samuel Clemens (Mark Twain), *Life on The Mississippi.* Toronto: Dover Thrift Edition, 2000, Chapter 4.

46

riverboat cruise. Hattie wanted to be seen in the company of Jenny Lind. Keeping up appearances exacts a heavy price. Back home in Pittsburgh on East Liberty Avenue, the MacDuncans had furnished their home with Jenny Lind furniture. The shapely well-turned legs of Jenny Lind chairs titillated Hattie's chatter over teacups, while Archibald dozed. When the MacDuncans went out and about in Pittsburgh they rode in a Jenny Lind carriage, a jaunty box-buggy with a fringe on the top.

So now aboard the cruise boat, Hattie MacDuncan blushed beet-red to have the famous Swedish operatic soprano within touching distance. A man shrouded under a cape with a black box on a tripod took their tintype picture with that new invention called the camera. "To think," gushed Hattie later to her envious friends in Pittsburgh, "to think that I was there with Jenny on the deck of the *Messenger II*. Captain Klinefelter was standing next to Jenny. What a tall, handsome man he is to grace the presence of such famous people as Jenny Lind and P. T. Barnum."

Captain John Klinefelter

"Schmoozing" means to converse casually, especially in order to gain an advantage or make a social connection. In Hebrew it meant 'to start a rumor.' A business person engages in schmoozing with potential clients at an evening party over *hors d'oeuvres* and drinks; a game of golf the next morning may clinch the deal. In 1840, schmoozing in America often took place on luxurious riverboats. Cruising down the river about five miles per hour[28] offered the opportunity to meet new people and greet old acquaintances. CEO's of developing American industry in the 1840s would have time in the Grand Saloon to make a sizeable purchase order, to contract to build a railroad to an outlying community, to electioneer for Abraham Lincoln as did Mark Twain to have his brother appointed Secretary of the Nevada Territory.

There was also offshore gambling. Many stories are told of the high stakes. Professional gamblers fleeced large sums of money from unsuspecting passengers. Sometimes the captains would break up the games, land the boat, and put the swindlers ashore.[29]

---

28 On 30 June 1870, the *SS Robert E. Lee* raced the *SS Natchez* from New Orleans, Louisiana to St Louis, Missouri—a distance of 675 miles. Speeding along at 7.5 miles per hour, the *Lee* arrived 5.5 hours ahead of the *Natchez*.

29 Arthur E. Hopkins, *Steamboats...on The Ohio and Mississippi Rivers.* Louisville, KY: Filson Club, 1943.

Steamboat Grand Saloon

Samuel Clemens (Mark Twain) was a Steersman under Captain John Klinefelter, Skipper of the *SS Pennsylvania*. Klinefelter had moved from the Ohio River to the Mississippi run from St. Louis to New Orleans. They made a few trips together. Twain was "learning the river."

When Captain Klinefelter called for depth soundings in the river, he gave the command with a signal from the whistle. Clemens took soundings when necessary from both sides of the boat. One signal from Klinefelter in the wheel house sent Clemens to the starboard (right) side, two signals to the port side (left). Soundings were taken when making a crossing, going through rapids, or whenever there was doubt as to the depth of the water.

There was a certain silence to the huge palace of a steamboat passing imperceptibly through the dark waters. The thrusting steam pistons propelled the paddle wheels noiselessly in the silent night. Captain Klinefelter listened to the musical chanting of Samuel Clemens' lyrical voice. The musical mode of *Quarter Less Twain* meant a depth of ten and one-half feet. When Klinefelter heard Clemens sing out *"Mark Twain*, it signified two fathoms (twelve feet).

Mark Twain Notes

Captain Klinefelter listened hopefully for *No Bottom* indicating a depth of more than 24 feet. A boat kept in deep water avoided the danger of going aground.[30] A local tradition has it that on that famous trip with P. T. Barnum and Jenny Lind, the *SS Messenger II* went aground briefly on a sandbar at Old Town; local folk point vaguely at a sandy riverine area remembered as Jenny Lind Bar.

Samuel Clemens achieved his own license to pilot riverboats. He quit the *SS Pennsylvania* but not before he got a job for his brother on board. It was a sad employment opportunity if Clemens could have foreseen what happened on 13 June 1858.

Riverboats were powered by steam boilers. The *SS Pennsylvania* had four boilers that needed to be monitored all the time. In those days, there were no electronic sensors to warn that the steam pressure had reached its limits. The chief engineer was supposed to be keeping an eye on these four belching behemoths. Instead, he was watching something else. His eyes were drawn to the many pretty women promenading the deck. So witnesses later said.

The boilers exploded.

Mark Twain described the scene:

---

[30] Mary Wheeler, *Steamboatin' Days - Folks Songs of the River Packet Era.* Louisiana State University Press, 1944.

Many people were flung to considerable distances and fell in the river; among these were Mr. Wood and my brother and the carpenter. The carpenter was still stretched upon his mattress when he struck the water seventy-five feet from the boat. Brown, the pilot, and George Black, chief clerk, were never seen or heard of after the explosion. The barber's chair, with Captain Klinefelter in it and unhurt, was left with its back overhanging vacancy - everything forward of it, floor and all, had disappeared; and the stupefied barber, who was also unhurt, stood with one toe projecting over space, still stirring his lather unconsciously saying not a word.

Captain John Klinefelter and Steersman Mark Twain
served on the SS Pennsylvania

Captain John Klinefelter was the youngest brother of our great, great, great grandfather, Jesse. Five Klinefelter brothers were steamboat captains out of Pittsburgh—Michael, Thomas, Jesse, Jacob and John.[31]

Captain Jesse Klinefelter was skipper of the *SS Hibernia II* from 1848 to 1849. His interstate river route followed the valleys from Pittsburgh, Pennsylvania to Wheeling, West Virginia. There

---
31

the Ohio River turns south for a hundred miles with industrial West Virginia on its east bank and the State of Ohio on its west. At Rockport, West Virginia, the Ohio River veers west and wanders aimlessly two hundred miles to Cincinnati, Ohio and then another hundred meandering miles to Louisville, Kentucky. Two hundred further miles along the Ohio, the SS *Hibernia II* reached Paducah, Kentucky. [32] There Captain Jesse took a left upstream on the Cumberland River to Nashville, Tennessee for another two hundred miles. Captain Jesse's journey enjoyed shorelines of beauty and faraway vistas of forested mountains.

On his final journey, Captain Jesse Klinefelter died while returning to his homeport of Pittsburgh on 6 May 1849. Born on 3 February 1815, he died at the age of 34. Jesse was a victim of cholera that claimed the lives of many of his passengers on that fateful cruise. According to the *Cincinnati Library Records*, "Jesse Klinefelter died . . . while piloting the *Hibernia II Steamboat* when she was landing with cholera aboard." Jesse's youngest brother, John later piloted the *SS Messenger II*.

---

32 The Ohio River flows west from Paducah to Cairo, Illinois where it joins the Mississippi River.

Anne Rue Brooks sketched by her grandson, J S Klinefelter

Anne Rue Brooks was born on 15 December 1822. Jesse Klinefelter was born on 3 February 1815 at Baltimore, Maryland, the son of Jacob Klinefelter and Susan Miller. Anne Rue Brooks married Jesse Klinefelter on 7 January 1840. Anne and Jesse parented five children:

Joseph G. 20 March 1842—19 November 1911 – our great great grandfather

Mary Elizabeth 14 May 1843—15 April 1844

Susetta 10 November 1844—26 May 1847

Judge Sharpless 8—July 1846—28 May 1905

George Jesse 28 August 1848—7 June 1872

The three sons of Anne and Jesse Klinefelter served in the Civil War—Joseph, Judge and George. Their father, Jesse had died in 1849 before the Civil War broke out. Their mother, Anne died on 26 September 1901 at Pittsburgh.

Civil War Battles

Joseph G. Klinefelter fought in major battles of the
Civil War as an Artificer of Cannons.

Joseph G. Klinefelter

Joseph Klinefelter's Civil War

"With malice toward none, with charity for all, with firmness in the right, as God gives us to see the right, let us strive on to finish the work we are in, to bind up the nation's wounds, to care for him who shall have borne the battle, and for his widow and his orphan - to do all which may achieve and cherish a just and lasting peace among ourselves and with all nations."

—Abraham Lincoln

After filing the saw teeth along the right side of the blade, and reversing the saw to file the obverse side, Joseph Klinefelter paused with his hands still poised with his tool. Looking through his workshop window, his eyes adjusted to rest on the boy planing an axe handle. Joseph was a carpenter and his teenage son was apprenticed to him to learn the trade. Together they were platform framing a new house in the East Liberty section of Pittsburgh. They would build many houses in East Liberty. Joseph kept a meticulous workshop—a trait he would pass on to his son, Judge Sharpless Klinefelter.

"What did you do in the Civil War, Dad?" his son asked. Soldiers who have suffered the heat of battle are often reluctant so speak about it. Joseph was no exception. The military record of the Union Army indicates that he served in many major battles of the Civil War.[33]

A decade had passed since the last shot was fired and Joseph had recently been elected Commander of the GAR in Pittsburgh.[34] His father's recent notoriety caused his son to ask.

"I fixed the cannons. I was called the Artificer of the Cannons."
"What are cannons?"
"Big guns mounted on wheels that shoot balls at the enemy."
"Like the one in the front of the Legion Post?"
"Yes. That's a Civil War cannon."

"Did you fire the cannons?
"Well. Yes. That was primarily what I did. I loaded and fired the cannons."

---

[33] Military record: *Allegheny County, Pennsylvania, in the war for the suppression of the rebellion, 1861-1865: roll of honor, defenders of the flag, attack on Fort Sumter, S.C., April 12, 1861, surrender at Appomattox, Va., April 9, 1865* — Klinefelter, Joseph G.. Private

[34] GAR = Grand Army of the Republic J.B. McPherson Post #117 in Pittsburgh.

"Were soldiers killed?"

Joseph looked at his son with an awkward grimace. After a long pause, he gave a short nod. It was a heavy question. A question most soldiers don't want to talk about.

"And **ar·TIF·i·cer**?" the boy persisted in his questioning.

"Artificer is a fancy word for a craftsman. It comes from the word *artisan*—a worker who builds or fixes things."

"So you and I build houses. Are we **AR·ti·sans**?"

"You could say that. A carpenter is an artisan."

The conversation lagged and Joseph finished setting the teeth on his saw. With a sharp saw like that, his son would one day accidentally lose parts of two fingers.

Decades later, when J.S.Klinefelter, an octogenarian, was talking to us his great grandsons, he continued that line of thought. "No. A sharp saw can be counted on to do its task!" Grandpa K asserted. "It is a dull saw that causes one to lose fingers." He held up his two cut off fingers.

Some months later Joseph's son, Judge, would be asked to draw a map of the Civil War at school. He drew it on his father's drafting table in the workshop. Joseph was sharpening another saw but he watched his son's progress with the cartography.

Battle after battle, march after march, month after month, the son began to realize the extent of his father's involvement in the worst conflict in American history.[35]

"So you fought at the Battle of Bull Run?"

---

[35] Swafford Johnson, *Great Battles of the Civil War.* East Bridgewater, MA: JGPress, 2012.

"Right after I enlisted on 16 August 1862. We lost 10,000 men."

"Shiloh?"

"Those were two bad days. We lost 13,000 men."

"The Battle on The Bridge over Antietam Creek?"

"Over a creek that emptied into the Potomac. My leg was wounded and I was captured."

His son fell silent with those words. But then he asked his father, "What do you feel when you are shot?"

Joseph halted his file in mid thrust.

"At first," he hesitated. "At first you don't feel anything. But you know something has happened to your leg. And then…."

"And then?" his son encouraged his words.

"Then you feel the pain and see the blood."

His son looked deeply into his father's face.

Joseph continued. "The Battle on The Bridge over Antietam Creek was worth it."

"Worth it?"

"Yes. After Antietam, Abe Lincoln got up the courage to give the Emancipation Proclamation.

"The Emancipation Proclamation?"

"This is what Abraham Lincoln said. He said: *"all persons held as slaves within any State shall be then, thenceforward, and forever free!"*

"That is what Abraham Lincoln said. That is what he said. *All slaves shall be free.*"

The boy listened silently as his pencil continued to map the war.

Joseph continued, "The Confederates put me in Libby Prison. But I guess they didn't want to deal with my leg. A week later, the 6th of October, there was a prisoner exchange at Aiken's Landing below Dutch Gap in Virginia. 3021 Union soldiers were exchanged for 3000 Confederate soldiers. I was one of the Union soldiers exchanged. I managed to get home to Pittsburgh. I needed some time to recover. That was when your Mother and I decided to get married. And on the 26th of November we did."

"Did you go back into the war?"

"Of course. I went back in January."

"Were you okay?"

"Well yes. We walked endlessly. It was a war that never quit."

"How was that?"

"At the end of October we were clear down in Tennessee. I was wounded again at Wauhatchie. They took me west to the hospital at Nashville. Would you believe, they charged me $13.85 to transport me 130 miles? I was laid up for nine months!"

"But you went back?" the boy looked inquiringly into his father's eyes.

"Peach Tree Creek near Atlanta in July. I marched with General Sherman from Chattanooga to Atlanta. We were on a high hill overlooking Atlanta when we took the city.[36] You were born on the day that I was firing the cannon on that hill. 22 July 1864."

The boy was silent.

But his father was building to the conclusion of his story.

"Then we marched onward all the way to Savannah by the sea. There were 60,000 of us and we cut a swath 60 miles wide. The idea was to break the South's will to continue the

---

36 The Jimmy Carter Presidential Center is located on the hill where General Sherman ended the Civil War.

war. We split the Confederacy in two and the North re-elected Abraham Lincoln."[37]

---

[37] **Joseph G. Klinefelter soldier and artificer of cannons**
16 August 1862 enlisted in the army
28 August appears at Independent Battery E
17 September 1862 wounded and captured at Battle of Antietam Bridge (Sharpsburg, Maryland)
28 September 1862 confined at Libby Prison, Richmond, Virginia.
6 October 1862 paroled at Aikens Landing, Virginia
5 November 1862 reported at Camp Parole, Maryland
26 November 1862 married Caroline Stetler at Pittsburgh
November & December 1862 absent from the ranks/muster roll
January 1863 present at muster
29 October 1863 wounded at the Battle of Wauhatchie, and taken to the hospital at Nashville, transport charge $13.85
November-December until July 1864 absent from muster rolls
19-20 July 1864 Battle of Peachtree Creek
22 July—25 August 1864 Occupation of Atlanta, Georgia under General William Tecumseh Sherman
November-December 1864 March to the sea under General Sherman cutting the Confederacy in two

Judge S Klinefelter F   Joseph G Klinefelter GF

Emma Ackermann Klinefelter M   Elizabeth Mason Stackhouse Brooks
GGGM   Anne Rue Brooks Klinefelter Hendrikson GGM

Blanche Mabel Klinefelter   Caroline Klinefelter GM

Joseph and Caroline had an unexpected newcomer to their home. Blanche Mabel Klinefelter was born on 27 September 1887 in Pittsburgh to their son, Judge S. Klinefelter and his wife, Emma Ackermann. A year later, Blanche lost her mother 30 Dec 1888 in childbirth complicated by pneumonia. Blanche was raised in the home of her grandparents, Caroline Stetler and Joseph Klinefelter. Her father, J. S. Klinefelter, worked to support the household; seven years later he married Lois Bethia Campbell and by her had two more daughters—Caroline in 1896 and Hortense in 1898.

On 6 September 1910 on a visit to see his granddaughter, Blanche, and her family in Nebraska, Joseph Klinefelter penned these notes about his life and gave them to her. The following year on 19 November 1911, Joseph died.

"I, Joseph G. Klinefelter, am of Pittsburgh, in the State of Pennsylvania where I was born on 20 March 1842. As near as I can recollect, my Grandfather on my Mother's side was born in Philadelphia, Pennsylvania. His name was Joshua Brooks by profession a Blacksmith. He lived to a good old age.

"My Grandmother, Elizabeth Mason Brooks, was born on 19 March 1802 in Philadelphia, Pennsylvania and died on 5 September 1901. She was 99 years.

"My Mother's name was Anne R. Brooks. She had three brothers—Steven, Henry, and Samuel; and two sisters— Emma and Sarah who died the fourth of last month (4 August 1910). The other sister, Emma, the last of the family is still living.

"My Mother was married to a Steamboat Pilot who steamboated from Pittsburgh, Pennsylvania to Cincinnati, Ohio to Nashville, Tennessee on the Ohio and Cumberland Rivers. His name was Jesse Klinefelter. My Mother had five children to him—Susetta, Mary Elizabeth, Joseph G., Judge S., and George J. All of my family were born in Pittsburgh, Pennsylvania.

"My Grandfather was born in Germany. I also remember my Grandmother on my Father's side. She died when I was about 4 or 5 years old. She had six boys—Joseph, John, Thomas, Jacob, Michael, and Jesse; and one girl—Eve. All the boys but Joseph were Pilots and Steamboat Captains.

"I, Joseph G. Klinefelter, married Caroline Stetler of Philadelphia, Pennsylvania on 26 November 1862. We had one son born to us, Judge S. Klinefelter, on 22 July 1864 in Pittsburgh. (At this time Joseph G. Klinefelter served in the Civil War as a Union Soldier. He was wounded and imprisoned in Libby Prison in Richmond, Virginia. He was allowed to return to Pittsburgh where he was hospitalized for many months.) In 1867 we moved to 5612 Harvard Street in the East Liberty part of Pittsburgh. I and my son, Judge S. Klinefelter, were House Carpenters and helped to build a great many houses in East Liberty where we have lived for 43 years."

Gary Arthur Thomson visits Stetler graves at Augustus Lutheran Church, Trappe, Pennsylvania.

The church is the oldest continuous Lutheran congregation in America.

Caroline Stetler Klinefelter

Caroline's Lineage to The Bell

A bell's not a bell 'til you ring it!
—Oscar Hammerstein II

Caroline Stetler Klinefelter was our great great grandmother. Through Caroline came the lineage of the Liberty Bell. It came through Great Grandpa Klinefelter's mother, Caroline Stetler. Not through his father, Joseph Klinefelter.

William Hurrie & Mary
|
Margaret Hurrie & John McGinley
|
Ann McGinley & Christian Stetler
|
Abner Stetler & Caroline Garrison
|
Caroline Stetler & Joseph Klinefelter
|
Judge S. Klinefelter & Emma Ackermann
|
Blanche Klinefelter & Herbert J. Thomson

From Oetz we drove up the Otztal Valley to where the road ended. Then we walked. A cow path led through Alpine meadows where mountain flowers dotted the grass. Above us huge drifts of snow clung precariously to the jagged rocks. We paused to watch an avalanche of snow break from a faraway peak and cascade with the sound of thunder into the crevices below. A seasoned skier in our group tells us how she survived being covered by the snow of an avalanche.

Finally we reached the mountain pass where Oetzi, the man in the ice, was discovered in September 1991. Those who found Oetzi at first thought he was a recent storm victim, a skier who had succumbed to a blizzard. Upon closer observation, they saw that Oetzi was wearing sandals knitted and bound from grasses. His two capes were also made from grasses. Archaeologists soon determined that his copper axe pre-dated the Bronze and Iron Ages. Further laboratory tests dated Oetzi to 5300 years ago. Oetzi died and was freeze-dried before the Pyramids were built! Caught in a niche under the ice, Oetzi had been preserved 53 centuries until recent global warming released his body from the glacial ice and snow.

Scientists took Oetzi's DNA. They compared it with the growing DNA data-bank of European peoples. What do you know? An Irish lady from Cork has the DNA so akin to Oetzi that she could be his daughter!

Oetzi is not just another "old fossil." *National Geographic* called Oetzi the most significant archaeological discovery ever because we all see ourselves linked to this human being who lived 5300 years ago! Oetzi makes dull paleontology and boring anthropology come alive! Oetzi is real!

Today one can stand at the grave of William Hurrie with a 13-star flag of Colonial America and think about one's bloodline coming down the generations from this man. It is not 5300 years ago, but it is still mind-boggling to think about. Could the links of the family tree be sorted out for seven, eight, nine or ten generations? Even eleven?

Dean Ackermann Thomson has spent years prodigiously sifting through the genealogical material found on gravestones, in family Bibles, in immigration logs, in government archives, in war records, in diaries, in personal letters, and in attics. His efforts reward us with historic connections that link us back to the man who rang the Liberty Bell in Philadelphia in 1776. Incredibly, this family tradition has spin-off details from Colonial America.

The lineage laid out at the beginning of this chapter walks us back to Old Pine Church in Philadelphia where the Hurrie's and the McGinley's are memorialized, to Augustus Lutheran Church in Trappe, Pennsylvania where the story continues with at least two generations of the Stetler's. Our journey into the past continues in Pittsburgh where threads merge in a confluence of connections.

Emma, Blanche & J.S. Klinefelter in March 1888

Emma Ackermann Klinefelter

Emma Ackermann's Family Saga

While every refugee's story is different and their anguish personal, they all share a common thread of uncommon courage to survive, to persevere and to rebuild their shattered lives.

—Antonio Guterres, UN High Commissioner for Refugees

Emma Ackermann was our great grandmother. Emma was born on 28 August 1863 in Pittsburgh, Pennsylvania. Emma married Judge Sharpless Klinefelter. They had a daughter, Blanche Mabel Klinefelter. Emma died on 30 December 1888 during childbirth complicated by pneumonia. She was only 25 years of age.

Emma's parents came as refugees from Germany. Michael Ackermann was born in Darmstadt, Germany in the southern part of Hesse-Darmstadt Province on 31 December 1832. His father was Adam Ackermann. Adam is our first documented ancestor of the Ackermann's.

Darmstadt was the epicenter of a German social revolution that failed. The German common people sought the same freedom that had been won in America in 1776 and France in 1789. Wealthy *ober-klassen* Germans scoffed at freedom and justice for all. In a patronizingly superior manner, these privileged patricians said that the peasantry should not rise above their station. In fact these rich *Plutokraten* taxed the poor even more. To make matters worse, the condescending German-Prussian military class conscripted poor youth to soldier their war making. Michael lived where he could see the soldiers marching in the streets. Darmstadt was close to Baden where the draft board made up the lists. Baden was where the warrants for arrest were written. Local Politzei enforced the rules of the Reich.

In 1849, the year after the Peasants' Revolt failed, Michael Ackermann left Germany. He was only sixteen, a ripe age for conscription into the army. Michael abandoned Germany and sought his fortune in the New World. He left his native land, made the long journey across the Atlantic, and alighted in Pennsylvania. There were many German immigrants in Pittsburgh. Hopes were running high in America, and Michael had high expectations. Settling down in Pittsburgh, Michael remained there the rest of the innovative and consequential 19th Century.

In the New World, Michael would become Eliza Wittmer's husband.

Emma's mother was Elizabeth Wittmer Ackermann. Eliza, as she was called, was born on 2 November 1837 in Dettighofen, in Baden Province of Germany. Eliza was 10 years old when her mother died. Her young life was difficult in a destitute household. Her father, Xaver Wittmer was a poor farmer who also tried his hand at tailoring and mining without much success. They were living an impoverished life near the little village of Dettighofen. Xaver's oldest son, George, was required to register for the draft. Under the threat of conscription into the German-Prussian Army, Xaver may have urged his son to emigrate.

Eliza Wittmer, 10 years old, was caring for her siblings with difficulty. In March of 1854, George took his sister, Eliza, and fled to America. When the police couldn't locate them, their names went on the "wanted list." They were stripped of citizenship and fined 800 Gulden. But George and Eliza were long gone. The authorities may have threatened George and Eliza's father, Xaver. In those dangerous times, many parents went bankrupt paying the heavy fines of their refugee children.

WANTED WARRANT

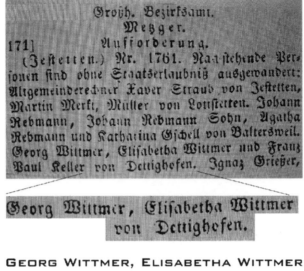

Großh. Bezirksamt.
Mezger.
171]   Aufforderung.
(Zeftetten.) Nr. 1761. Nachstehende Personen sind ohne Staatserlaubniß ausgewandert: Allgemeinderednar Xaver Straub von Zeftetten, Martin Merkt, Müller von Lonftetten. Johann Rebmann, Johann Rebmann Sohn, Agatha Rebmann und Karharina Gschell von Baltersweil. Georg Wittmer, Elifabetha Wittmer und Franz Paul Keller von Dettighofen. Ignaz Grießer,

Georg Wittmer, Elifabetha Wittmer von Dettighofen.

GEORG WITTMER, ELISABETHA WITTMER
. . . VON DETTIGHOFEN.

Arrest Warrant for Georg and Elisabetha Wittmer

George Wittmer did not take his emigration decision lightly. From humble beginnings, George Wittmer succeeded in making the American dream come true. American was a land of opportunity. With hard work, George founded the Wittmer Ice Company, the Wittmer Brick Company and the American Natural Gas Company. The Pennsylvania portion of American Natural Gas Company was sold to John D. Rockefeller of Standard Oil of New Jersey in 1926!

A half a century later, George Wittmer returned to Dettighofen where he built a library! On 7 May 1905, George dedicated the *Wittmer-Bibliothek*—a public library. George built the library, paid for the library, and paid for the large collection of books. He provided money in trust to sustain that library. Only recently have his funds run out and the library is being sustained in other ways.

The Wittmer-Bibliothek that George Wittmer built in Dettighofen

George remembered how the rich German aristocracy had treated peasant children when he was a child. Only the wealthy with their private schools got an education. Public education an absolute necessity for a democracy—was unknown in the feudalistic atmosphere of Germany. Poor children were serfs providing child labor without regard for health, education or childhood happiness.

Dettighofen is a beautiful German hamlet on the southern edge of the Black Forest. Dettighofen is land-locked in a Swiss horseshoe. Crossing and then re-crossing the Swiss border is complicated and expensive. The Swiss guard $32,000,000,000,000 untaxed dollars of the richest 0.001 per cent of the world's population. Dettighofen is a stone's throw from Davos. Each year at Davos, the world leaders of the richest 0.001 per cent gather to make "austerity plans" for the remaining 99.9%.

Under the progressive Republican president, Dwight Eisenhower, there was a graduated tax system; the very rich paid 93% tax and did not complain. In the Eisenhower era, America employed thousands of people to build infrastructure including the Interstate Highway System.[38]

Presidents for the last three decades have cut taxes for the wealthy.[39] President Clinton de-regulated the banks to speculate with ordinary peoples' bank accounts and home mortgages. The tax cuts of the rich created a titanic disequilibrium between the rich and everybody else. The 0.001 per cent have accumulated 32 TRILLION untaxed dollars! You can't drive directly to Dettighofen. You have to go 50 miles around the fortified Swiss horseshoe to get to the land-locked village. And so it goes.[40]

Xaver Wittmer, our great great great grandfather, never could get ahead in Dettighofen. He tried his hand at farming, tailoring, and mining. The 0.001 per cent in Dettighofen labeled Xaver a ne'er-do-well. But when Xaver came to America, he discovered a more level playing field. In America, Xaver succeeded!

The village of Dettighofen itself is picture perfect. Painted frescoes adorn quaint cottages. In the Jura foothills, the local golf course overlooks the Rhine River. Waterfalls cascade down into the gorge. Persecuted French Protestants, Huguenots, fled here before emigrating to New Paltz, New York. Aggrieved Mennonites and Anabaptists sought refuge in this region.

---

38 Robert B. Reich, *Aftershock: The Next Economy and America's Future*. New York: Vintage, 2011.

39 Haynes Johnson, *Sleepwalking Through History*. New York: Anchor Books, 1992.

40 *Sympatico News*, 22 July 2012. The IMF (International Monetary Fund) and the World Bank estimate that the wealthy 0.001 per cent shelter $32 trillion in untaxed assets that create the real crisis in the world economy.

Eliza & her son George Washington Ackermann visited
Dettighofen in 1903 aboard the *Kroonland*

After months of living dangerously, George and Eliza arrived
in America and settled in Pittsburgh, Pennsylvania. Year's later
Eliza's son, George Washington Ackermann wrote a tribute to his
mother's bravery:

> *... so far away, your valued life began.*
> *Your childhood's days were sweet, but short,*
> *Marred all too soon by death's cold dart*
> *Hurled at your dear mother....*
> *In the brave effort to earn your way*
> *And help maintain the family sway....*
> *Scarce had girlhood's age begun*
> *Until you turned to setting sun*
> *A better home to find....*
> *You blazed the way for others' good;*
> *Loneliness and homesickness withstood....*
> *In this new strange land....*

Eliza's brother, George Wittmer wrote back to their father, Xaver Wittmer, in Germany and tried to persuade him to follow him to the New World. On 24 January 1857, Xaver Wittmer turned in the request for emigration to America at the regional office in Jestetten, Germany. He had to give up his German citizenship. He had 1500 Florins of maternal inheritance and owned a small property. With his daughter, Kunigunde, and son, Xavier II, Xaver Wittmer sailed from Le Harvre, France on the lower deck of the *Edward Stanley*. They arrived in New York City in May 1857. The family was re-united.

In his sixties, Xaver, the ne'er-do-well of Dettighofen became a rich man in Pennsylvania. In 1857, his son, George, purchased land on Middle Road, Shaler Township, where he built a small frame house. During the American Civil War much land lay untilled; Xaver may have invested in land. Xaver died in 1886; he had spent 29 good years in the American land of opportunity and it had treated him well.

George Washington Ackermann & Eliza Ackermann

Michael Ackermann & Elisabetha (Eliza) Wittmer were united in Holy Matrimony in Pittsburgh on 5 October 1862.

Eight children were born to Eliza and Michael—Emma, Elise, George Washington, Charles, Louisa, Ida and two who died in infancy. George Washington Ackermann was born on George Washington's birthday. Emma would be our great grandmother.

At the end of their lives Michael and Eliza were running a "mom and pop" grocery. Michael died on 24 August 1900. George Washington Ackermann accompanied his mother in August 1903 on a journey back to Dettighofen. Eliza died on 4 July 1910 on the 134th anniversary of her adopted homeland.

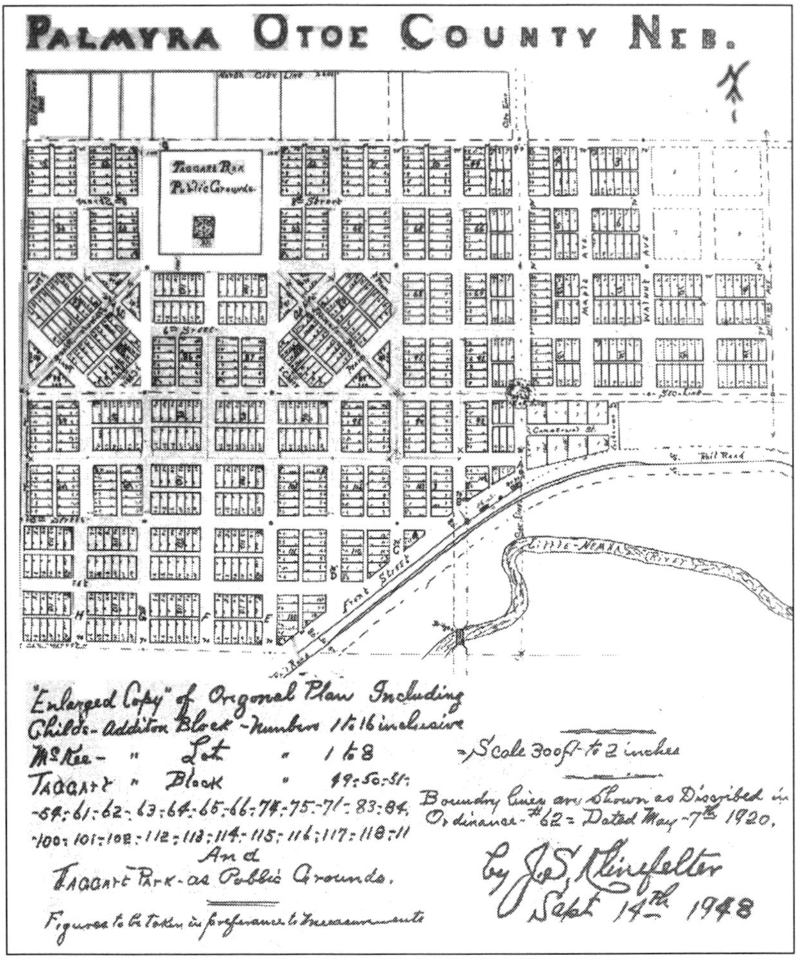

Palmyra Nebraska Town Plan by J S Klinefelter 1948

Gary Arthur Thomson   Arthur Klinefelter Thomson
Kimberly Ann Thomson
Blanche Klinefelter Thomson   Judge Sharpless Klinefelter 1960

Epic of Great Grandpa Klinefelter

"He was a Renaissance Man."

Great Grandpa Klinefelter when he came to live with his family in Nebraska was in the last two decades of a century-long life. J.S. Klinefelter was a stately gentleman who would tolerate no nonsense. At eighty he was more energetic than most men who are thirty-something. Grandpa Klinefelter, as we called him, was a person who moved mountains and had no leeway with laziness.

When President Eisenhower brought the Liberty Bell to Lincoln, Nebraska, Grandpa Klinefelter had the whole family present for the opening. We waved American flags. Grandpa held a press conference and debated with an impudent reporter about William Hurrie who rang this amaranthine Liberty Bell in 1776. The "aw-shucks" reporter confessed that he found history boring. "Just a bunch of dates." Grandpa Klinefelter went into overdrive and took a bypass to the *Lincoln Journal and Star*. He submitted a "proper article" which the newspaper printed in full.

Grandpa Klinefelter discovered that Palmyra, Nebraska had been *a planned village* by its founder John Taggart in 1870. John Taggart was of the same vintage as Sir Ebenezer Howard who wrote the classic, *Garden Cities of Tomorrow*. Howard was one of the most influential pioneers in the field of urban planning. Both men envisioned utopian communities in which people lived harmoniously together with nature. Ebenezer Howard emigrated to Nebraska in 1871. Both of these town planners associated with the new American dream of Walt Whitman, Ralph Waldo Emerson, and Henry David Thoreau.

Grandpa Klinefelter discovered Taggart's town plan for Palmyra! He was ecstatic! Being an architectural engineer, he proceeded to draw a large rendering of the town plan of Palmyra. The banker was so impressed that he put it on the great wall of the Bank of Palmyra. Palmyra had been laid out on the English gridiron plan with diagonal streets leading to the central park. The park was named appropriately Taggart Park.

Then Grandpa went aground with the recalcitrant town board. Grandpa wanted to follow the Taggart plan and put in sidewalks. So Grandpa paved his own sidewalk according to John Taggart's specifications. Later, Gerald Royal, a kindred spirit with Grandpa Klinefelter, wanted to pave the Palmyra streets according to the Taggart plan; once again the town board reneged.

Below the town on the flood plain of the Little Nemaha Creek, earliest Palmyrans laid out a horse racetrack. Great Uncle Alec liked to show us where the racetrack fence bordered his farm. He pointed out that the fence wire had no barbs. Ordinarily barbwire was used to fence cattle in. But the racetrack required no barbs to harm the galloping horses. The old man pointed at the barbless fence wire that he had installed some sixty years earlier. Ancient growth encased the wire as though it had pierced the tree trunks. At eighty-something, Uncle Alec continued to hoe sunflowers, cockle burrs, and button weeds while recalling the days when "this was all prairie grass." On one of his farms, Uncle Alec stipulated that forty acres remain as prairie as when he grazed cattle there for 50¢ a month as a boy. [41]

Great Uncle Alec was Grandpa Klinefelter's contemporary in age, both had been born during the Civil War. They celebrated their July birthdays together each summer with their extended family.

---

[41] Willa Cather, *O Pioneers!* Boston: Houghton Mifflin, 1913, p. 1. Willa Cather, *My Antonia*. New York: Dover, 1995. Growing up in Red Cloud, Willa Cather's Nebraska novels describe the prairie and its people.

Woodcut of J. S. Klinefelter in 1891 at age 27

Judge Sharpless Klinefelter was born in Pittsburgh, Pennsylvania on 22 July 1864.[42] On that very day, his father, Joseph, was activating his cannon at the Siege of Atlanta that began on the 22nd and settled the Civil War. General Sherman marched with 60,000 soldiers from Chattanooga through Georgia.

J.S. boasted that when he was a boy that he had a bicycle and delivered newspapers to Andrew Carnegie (1835-1919)—the great industrialist of America's most industrial city.

He was a toddler when his father came home from the war. In those months he watched his father re-integrate into the family routine. Months had turned into years of living in pup tents on Civil War battlefields. And after the battles, the cannon in his keeping was always in need of repair for the next encounter. That was risky after-dark work that made a cannon artificer skittish to

---

[42] The 1864 Directory of Pittsburgh, page 171, shows Joseph G. Klinefelter, carpenter, living at 42 Chestnut, and that is the address of Abner Stetler, his father-in-law. Apparently Joseph and Caroline lived with her parents during the Civil War period and their son was born there on 22 July 1864.

say the least. The toddler heard his father startled awake by the sound of the striking clock in the otherwise silence of the night. War is not easy to get over, if ever. Those politicians who talk so easily about going to war have often never been under fire.

J.S. grew up with disciplined carpentry. His father's shop was meticulous. Tools were always in their place. The workbench was cleaned up after every project. And the tools. Joseph G. Klinefelter never started a new project unless his tools were in top condition. In Ancient Egypt there were two tool sharpeners for every workman who used the tool to cut blocks for a pyramid. Archaeologists know this from the workshop middens in the vicinity of the pyramids. Joseph had more saw files than he had saws. And it was so in the life of his apprenticed son.

In the last twenty years of his life with us in Nebraska, J.S., Great Grandpa Klinefelter created no less than three complete workshops. When he first arrived, he put together a scrupulous carpenter's shop on the old Homestead where Blanche and Herb were then living. In that shop he looked fondly at the two 28 inch hard tire bicycles that he had sent to Blanche's children at the time of the First World War! And in another corner sat the Neracar Motorcycle that he had sent later. That Neracar had a sliding clutch/transmission and an automobile steering apparatus. At the Scottish Motorcycle Museum in Melrose, a Neracar is featured for its inventiveness.

At the far end of that little building on the Homestead, Grandpa K had installed a long workbench. Above it, he created a wall of tools—a row of wood chisels, a bank of handsaws, a cache of wood bits. His adjustable mitre box was fixed at the end of the bench so that he could cut from several positions.

The picture frames he mitred were exactingly straight, clean and unblemished.

Grandpa Klinefelter's woodwright shop contrasted with his family. We were accustomed to scattering our tools wherever they were used so that we could get back to the field. Having repaired a mower we needed to get back to cutting the alfalfa. There was so precious little sun time for curing the new mown hay. When we couldn't find our tools, Grandpa would say that sharpening and putting your tools away saves time and energy. "Don't throw effort after foolishness," he would admonish us with his no-nonsense face.

When he was "pushing ninety," Grandpa Klinefelter moved to Eagle, Nebraska to live alone. The town was ten miles away. He renovated an old schoolhouse for his lodging and his latest workshop! The local grocer, Jack Johanssen, approached him to install a frozen food locker next to his grocery store. Grandpa obliged. He understood refrigeration and insulation as well as carpentry.

When he was over ninety, he established his final workshop. His son-in-law, Herb, had died and his daughter, Blanche, was alone. Grandpa was invited by his grandsons to come and live with his daughter in her home in Palmyra across from Taggart Park.

This final workshop was across the alley from the most illustrious school superintendent that Palmyra ever had—Bernard Davis. As a disciplined basketball coach, Davis would practice various plays and set-ups months before he ever scrimmaged. He consistently took his teams to the state tournaments. Davis was also a top-notch math and science teacher. Both over six feet tall, Bernard Davis and J.S. Klinefelter were highly disciplined, no-nonsense self-starters. As such they got on famously across the alley. Sometimes their communication was only a word or a glance. But they knew each other's minds instinctively.

Emma Ackermann and J. S. Klinefelter

Emma Ackermann married Judge Sharpless Klinefelter in Pittsburgh on 25 October 1886. Their daughter, Blanche, was born on 27 September 1887. A second child was on the way when Emma contracted pneumonia. She and her babe died in childbirth. Emma was only twenty-five.

J.S. and his father were carpenters building houses in the East Liberty section of Pittsburgh. The three generations lived together with little Blanche growing up with her father, her Grandmother Caroline and her Grandfather Joseph.

Seven years later J.S. married Lois Bethia Campbell and by her had two more daughters—Caroline in 1896 and Hortense in 1898.

In 1900 a great fire burned through the downtown of Jacksonville, Florida. The railroad had recently been built from Pittsburgh to Jacksonville. J.S. was contracted as the outside foreman to supervise the construction of several buildings in central core of Jacksonville. He commuted back and forth to Pittsburgh when his work allowed. After Jacksonville, his work moved across the American South to as far west as Waco, Texas where he supervised the construction of a 40-story office building.

He gave a new dimension to our lives in Nebraska when this interesting man came to live in our midst. Early in his arrival, Dean Ackermann Thomson's father, Alfred, asked Great Grandpa Klinefelter to supervise the building of a new barn. It was fascinating to watch the barn plan staked out and the materials made ready. Grandpa marshaled the uncles and the cousins to do particular tasks.

When Grandpa Klinefelter returned to Palmyra to live with his daughter, Blanche, he was over ninety. One of his projects then was to build child-size rocking chairs for his great grandchildren. Another ambitious project was to produce several sturdy wagon boxes for farmers in the community including his grandsons.

When her family was at choir practice, Lorraine Thomson stayed with Grandma Blanche and Great Grandpa K. They played the game called Flinch. It was a huge deck of cards. Lorraine recalls that they never finished a game. When the pile had diminished to the last card, Grandpa K would reach out and turned the deck over to start anew. Lorraine said that it was longest Flinch game in history.

Judge Sharpless Klinefelter died in Palmyra when he was 100 years of age. He was still in top shape.

Herbert

City and Mills of Paisley, Scotland in 1850

"It was the best of times; it was the worst of times," Charles Dickens wrote in *A Tale of Two Cities.* Those words could be said for the Ronald family living in Paisley, Scotland in 1850. The Paisley weaving trade had been mechanized for greatly improved production, but the Industrial Revolution was at the expense of lost jobs for the working class of weavers. The Paisley print designs had achieved world renown, but the styles of women had suddenly shifted to bustles, and the Paisley shawl no longer could drape the figures of women to advantage. The decision of the Ronald family to emigrate to America was not easily made.

Margaret Ronald's Paisley Shawl in 1850

Margaret Ronald of Paisley, Scotland

Margaret Ronald was our great grandmother. Spirited and bright, Margaret was born in Paisley, Scotland on 15 October 1836. Her parents, Mary Gourley and Thomas Ronald II both of

Paisley, were married on 21 May 1820. According to the Paisley Census of 1841, Margaret's siblings were Mary, Agnes, William, John, and Thomas III. Jane and Robert came later.

Her grandfather, Thomas Ronald I started out as a smuggler—liquor, silk and tea from offshore ships and cattle on land. Learning the error of his ways, he was appointed an excise man with Robbie Burns; they collected taxes in Ayrshire. Thomas moved up in life when he married Margaret Stewart in the High Kirk of Paisley. That was in 1793. Thomas learned the flax dressing trade in a small thread spinning works and became a weaver of plain goods. Paisley weavers became famous for their Paisley Shawls that imitated expensive Cashmere shawls of the orient. Thomas never learned the fine art of weaving shawls.

When Margaret was turning twenty, her family emigrated from Scotland to America.

In the ancient cathedral for the Autumn Festival, two women demonstrated spinning and weaving in the old ways. They chanted and sang and counted as they worked with gusto. "We are weaving musical threads," they said! The cathedral resounded and smelled of the weaving trade. Penned little lambs signified wool. Spinners sat at spinning wheels beneath the stained glass windows; they spun the tufts of wool into long threads. Weavers at their looms were also part of the cathedral celebration. Little children nimbly aided the bobbins through the threads. Colored woven cloth draped the Lord's Table in the center of the cathedral. Light streamed in through the high windows to illuminate the finery displayed by the weavers. This harvest festival in the cathedral was symbolic of the daily work of the weavers of Strathclyde.

The Ronald's of Paisley were weavers. Indeed, weaving employed the whole region of Strathclyde. The wide Clyde Valley is indented with streams coming down from the hills. The streams powered the mills of mechanized weaving. In 1804, a Frenchman named Jacquard invented a loom that operated with a punch card system. It was a precursor to the binary computer! Handloom weavers had previously employed a child as a draw boy. Sitting atop the loom, Billy Ronald raised and lowered heddles attached to warp threads. The Jacquard loom eliminated the draw boy. The machine repeated the patterns with absolute conformity and the machine was 25 times faster. The Paisley cottage industry evolved into a factory process. It was called the Industrial Revolution. Jobs were lost. Like the Ronald family, many Scots emigrated to America—the land of opportunity.

In 1820, Paisley was a Scottish mill town that produced shawls like imported, expensive Cashmere's. A genuine Cashmere shawl cost £100. The cottage weavers of Paisley produced a similar shawl for £12 from local wool! The "place-name" of *Paisley* became the famous "brand-name" for shawls. *Paisley Shawls* were bright and colorful. Flowers and leaves intertwined in byzantine designs. Paisley was renowned for the intricacy of their shawl patterns. Then, with the bustle, the shawl went out of style. Furthermore, the mechanized Jacquard loom could produce a shawl for less than £1!

Claude Monet's painting of Madame Guadibert in a Paisley Shawl

Ystrad Clud is the river that named the Brythonic Kingdom of Strathclyde.[43] Ystrad Clud, Strath Cloyd, Srath Chluaidh, or Strath-Clyde are ancient cognomens for this lovely green land. Beginning as a fishing stream, Ystrad Clud meanders a hundred miles before cascading down the Falls of Clyde where its waters flow mightily through Glasgow into the Clydeside Shipyards.

---

43   Michael Lynch, *Scotland: A New History.* London: Pimlico, 1994, p. 12 ff.

The Firth of Clyde forms a waistline across Scotland to the Firth of Forth.

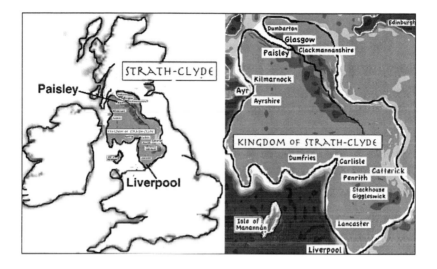

Brythonic Kelts inhabited these Lands. Spinning, weaving, milking, kneading, hoeing, eating, drinking, the Kelts of Strath-Clyde counted, rhymed and sang their way through life! Yan, tan, tether, mether, pimp, teezar, leezar, catterah, horna, dick—1 to 10. "*Old King Cole, a merry old soul*," ruled at Dun-Brython. King Arthur battled at Catterick and took a seat in Edinburgh. [44]

Dean Ackermann Thomson has researched government archives to discover the Ronald path from Paisley, Scotland to Poysippi, Wisconsin where family awaited. Dean found that instead of embarking from Glasgow, the Ronald's traveled to Liverpool to set sail! The Ronald's traversed the Kingdom of Strathclyde from Paisley in the north to Liverpool in the south. They traveled 250 miles over land in horse drawn carriages full

---

[44] Gary Arthur Thomson, *First Scots: Cruithni, Brythons, Gaels, Nords and Saxons*. New York: iUniverse, 2014.

of their worldly possessions. Along the way, they may have halted briefly to say goodbye to relatives and friends at Ayr, Mauchline, and Dumfries.

On 10 January 1850, some of Margaret's brothers, cousins, uncles and aunts sailed from Liverpool on the *Jamestown*. On this 1850 journey went her brothers—William Bunten Ronald, John Ronald, and Thomas Ronald III. Margaret's aunt, Mary Ronald Bunten, and her son, William Bunten, who of course was Margaret's cousin, accompanied them. Isabella and Thomas Shaw also were on board; Isabella was Margaret's cousin. They disembarked in New York City on 11 March 1850.

In 1856, our great grandmother, Margaret Ronald, sailed from Liverpool to New York on the *Franklin King*. She sailed with Thomas II and Mary Gourley Ronald, her parents. Mary and Jane were her sisters. Robert was her brother. They sailed for seven weeks on the Atlantic before arriving in New York City on 26 June 1856. From New York they made their way to Poysippi, Wisconsin where they joined their family.

Six months later the *Franklin King* sank in the icy waters of the Atlantic.

Clyde in Brythonic Keltic is pronounced Clud. In Gaelic Keltic it is Chluaidh. It is also written as Cloyd, which is closer to both the Brythonic and the Gaelic pronunciations. Dean Ackermann Thomson's brother carried the name of Cloyd. Cloyd was a generous and gentle person most worthy of his ancient Keltic name. It is fitting that Cloyd is buried on the original Homestead in Nebraska of Margaret Ronald of Strath-Cloyd.

Margaret and Arthur's first home had been in Nebraska City. Margaret operated a restaurant named The Western House was located across the street from the courthouse where the Old Grand Hotel used to stand and which is currently occupied by American National Bank.

Initially, Arthur worked as a carpenter for Alexander Majors building his freight wagons.

After that they moved to a dugout at a caravansary 35 miles west of Nebraska City.

In June 1864, Margaret and Arthur Thomson moved to their new log cabin on their Homestead. Dean Ackermann Thomson has an affidavit testifying that Arthur Reid Thomson and family had moved to the Homestead. Inspectors observed a log home 12 x 16 feet with one door and one window by creek. They also noted that Arthur had also started to construct the partial frame house measuring 15 x 17 feet that was 1½ stories tall. In addition, the homestead officials recorded a stable, cattle shed, log granary, root house-cellar, corncrib, rail crib and enough cut posts for 80 rods of fence. Cloyd Thomson is buried on that Homestead quite near the house of Margaret of Strath Cloyd.

Arthur continued working as a carpenter in Nebraska City to earn money. Every weekend he walked the 35 miles along the creeks of the Nemaha Watershed to their cabin in the roadless Nebraska Territory.

The locale acquired the name Paisley when Margaret's brother, Robert, applied to set up a post office. Eventually a school and church bore the name Paisley. William & Jane Bunten moved into their place on the acreage at Paisley in August 1865. Jane was Margaret's sister.

Margaret and Arthur's Homestead was two miles north of the Nebraska City Cut-Off of the Oregon Trail. In 1864, this new shortcut reduced the distance to Fort Kearney by almost a hundred miles. Being entrepreneurial, Margaret worked in the store along the trail. Her son, Alec worked in the store when he was not grazing cattle. Uncle Alec, that's how we knew our great uncle, often related stories of the prairie. Of course, there were no fences. So Alec was hired by neighbors to graze cattle on the open prairie for 50¢ per month. He recalled chewing a piece of Blue Stem Grass while watching the prairie chickens. He was still a very young boy and one day he took some baby skunks back to the cabin in his cap. He thought they were cute pets. Margaret had to use some precious tomato juice to give Alec a bath. With their father away, the little family was alone during the week in the cabin by the creek. Alec remembered the latchstring that his mother pulled in at night on the cabin door. Near the cabin was a burial mound of the Native People; people like the Oto and Pawnee still moved about the area that had been theirs since the Last Ice Age 13,000 years ago.

Margaret Ronald's great grandfather was George Ronald who was born in 1735. He married Janet Cameron Earn of Strathearn; Janet had a son, James, from previous marriage. George and Janet had four more children—Hector, Thomas I, William and Agnes.

Margaret Ronald's grandfather, Thomas I, lived in Ayrshire in the time of Robbie Burns, Scotland's most famous poet whose dates are 1759-1796. As the reader may recall, Thomas I smuggled liquor and cattle before becoming an excise man in Ayrshire.

Robbie Burns

The poet, Robbie Burns, was also a farmer and excise man in Ayrshire. Robbie is the poet who wrote those memorable lines:

O, wad some Power the giftie gie us
To see oursels as others see us!
It wad frae monie a blunder free us,
An' foolish notion

Burns wrote the poem, *The Ronalds in the Bennals*. *The Bennals* was a farm owned by William Ronald! In *Broad Scots*[45], Burns rhymed:

> *But ken ye the Ronalds that live in the Bennals?*
> *They carry the gree frae them a', man.*
> *Their father's a laird, and weel he can spare't:*
> *Braid money to tocher them a', man;*

Robbie Burns composed the epic poem, the *Jolly Beggars Cantata* at the local Poosie Nansies Pub in Mauchline, Ayrshire. The proprietor of this watering hole was none other than an Agnes Ronald who married Black Georgie Gibson. Robbie described the establishment as *"the favoured resort of lame sailors, maimed soldiers and vagabonds of that description."* The *Belle of Mauchline* was Jean Armour, Burns' wife.

Willie Ronald worked as a ploughman for Robbie Burns at his farm. About that time, Robbie Burns wrote *To A Mouse, On Turning Her Up In Her Nest With The Plough*. Robbie penned:

> *Wee, sleekit, cow'rin, tim'rous beastie,*
> *O, what a panic's in thy breastie!*
> *Thou need na start awa sae hasty,*
> *Wi'bickering brattle!*
> *I wad be laith to rin an' chase thee!*

---

45 *Broad Scots* is the language traditionally spoken by people living in the Lowlands of Scotland. *Broad Scots* is sometimes classified as a variety of English and sometimes as a separate language.

Robbie Burns captured the true spirit of Scotland. In the time of Margaret Ronald, the Scots had high hopes and great expectations.

Then let us pray that come it may,
(As come it will for a' that,)
That Sense and Worth, o'er a' the earth,
Shall bear *the gree, an' a' that.*
For a' that, an' a' *that,*
It's coming yet for a' that,
That Man to Man, the world o'er,
Shall brothers be for a' that.[46]

46 *Poems and Songs of Robert Burns*, edited by James Barke. Glasgow: Collins, 1960.

Dean Ackermann Thomson on Scottish Border with bagpiper

Arthur O' Scotland

Scotland! "Scotland the Brave! Alba an Aigh!" screak the bagpipes and drums! *How the Scots Invented the Modern World!* hypes a modern best seller.[47] Scots tend to be fiercely proud. Some say Scots have a superiority complex! Arthur Reid Thomson was no exception. He infixed his romantic sentiments into his family. On a melancholy day on the endless prairie, Arthur and Margaret recollected the glories of Scotland. In 1986 their grandson pilgrimaged to his grandparents' homeland; Arthur Klinefelter Thomson arrived at the Scottish border and literally kissed the ground!

---

47   Arthur Herman, How the Scots Invented the Modern World: The True Story of How Western Europe's Poorest Nation Created Our World & Everything in It. New York: Three Rivers Press. 2001

In the 1800s Edinburgh was the enlightened city of Europe. Edinburgh focalized science and intellectual thought. Adam Smith, James Hutton, David Hume, James Watt, Charles Darwin, Joseph Black, and Benjamin Franklin met at The Oyster Club to discuss science. James Hutton, the father of *geology*, articulated the geological strata of the headland near Edinburgh in his *Theory of The Earth*. Charles Darwin came to Edinburgh to present his findings on the *origins and evolution of living species*. Adam Smith, author of *Wealth of The Nations*, spelled out the *principles of capitalism*. Adam Ferguson pioneered historical *sociology*. James Watt described his *steam engines*. Benjamin Franklin visited the Oyster Club and talked about the use of *electricity*.

But, it was David Hume who had the most profound effect on America. David Hume was the philosopher of *pragmatism*. Hume, the Scot, gave America the gift of "*know how!*" Charles Saunders Pierce explained Hume's pragmatism in an article about *how things work*. John Dewey applied Hume's pragmatism to education; Dewey explained that children *learn by doing*. Pragmatically, William James broke away from European Gestalt psychology; James *applied psychology* to daily experience.

James Hutton said the Scottish discussions were "informal and amusing, despite their great learning." Certainly, Scottish science created the American pragmatic approach to solving problems and ultimately the American technological society. With a Scottish surname, General Stanley McChrystal recently said, "The special knack of Americans is *problem-solving*."

Modern clinical medicine was first practiced in Edinburgh. Before Edinburgh, dogmatic doctors pronounced the salvation of a disease without ever seeing the patient! Without examining the patient, the doctor imposed his cure at arm's length! Bloodletting was prescribed for just about everything in medieval European society. George Bernard Shaw called this ideological medicine "Heartbreak House."

During the Renaissance, Leonardo da Vinci carefully dissected plants, animals, and even human cadavers. He made meticulous drawings. Medieval doctors looked on with disdain. A few centuries later in Edinburgh, Leonardo's seeds began to grow. Doctors began to practice clinical medicine. Hands-on examinations and careful diagnosis preceded surgery or medical prescription.

But learning the new clinical procedure was not without its price! Interns studying to be doctors needed bodies to carve up and dissect to learn the clinical approach to medicine. It was the age of Charles Dickens. There were very rich people like Ebenezer Scrooge; and there were poor waifs like Tiny Tim and his desperate father, Bob Cratchit. In the class system of the Victorian Age, it was acceptable for medical students to kidnap, kill and carve up poor children—"for the greater good." So they said. Charles Dickens was describing the real world in the Age of Queen Victoria.

Arthur Reid Thomson and his brother Alexander were trudging up the dimly lit, seedy street called Leith Walk from the docks of Edinburgh.

A medical student came out of the shadows and grabbed Arthur. He pulled him under has long dark coat and was beginning to choke him to death. The young lad was a prime candidate for carving up.

Arthur's brother grabbed a loose brick from the street. He threw the brick crashing through the glass window of a store. The noise of shattering glass attracted attention. The medical student released his grasp on his struggling victim and ran off into the darkness.

So . . . Arthur Reid Thomson lived to tell the tale to his children. And it has been told from one generation to another to this very day.

Eilean Donan Castle near Kyle of Lochalsh

Arthur Reid Thomson was born on 1 January 1827. Arthur, his older sister Gennia, and his older brother Alexander were all born in Bannockburn—a small village suburb outlying the major city of Stirling. Bannockburn is famous in Scotland because it is the place where the Scots defeated the English. At the Battle of Bannockburn, Robert the Bruce led the Scots to victory over King Edward II of England on 23 June 1314.

Circumstantially in 1826 in the small village of Bannockburn, two Thomson brothers were hanged for stealing bread for their starving families. Charles Dickens bears witness that the poor were often hanged for stealing bread. The well-known Celtic song, *"The Fields of Athen Rye,"* portrays a family watching their father being taken away by the authorities for stealing a loaf of bread. The orphaned family sang, *"It's so lonely 'round the fields of Athen Rye."*

Arthur was his father's name, a stonemason. His mother was sick and soon thereafter died. Gennia married a man named Reid.

Arthur and Alexander were taken to Edinburgh to be raised by their grandparents who operated a coaching inn on the outskirts of the city. His grandfather had a stagecoach to shuttle passengers into Edinburgh from the inn.

Mons Meg Cannon at Castle above Edinburgh

A huge primitive canon called Mons Meg stood on the edge of the heights of Edinburgh by the Castle. Mons Meg had been fired at the English at the Battle of Flodden Field in 1513. The 20-inch barrel accommodated 400-pound cannon balls. From Edinburgh Castle, Mons Meg fired a cannon ball two measured miles. Sir Walter Scott had Mons Meg restored and placed at Edinburgh Castle.

Arthur Reid Thomson related to his children how his grandfather had lifted him up and placed him in the mouth of the famous cannon. He recalled looking out across the roofs of the city of Edinburgh. In 1960 Gary Arthur Thomson placed his two-years-old daughter Kimberly in the mouth so that she could view the city in the same way her great, great grandfather had done. Gary was a student at the University of Edinburgh. Shannon, the second daughter of Jeanette and Gary Thomson, was born at Eastern General Hospital on Leith Walk Hospital in Edinburgh on 28 December 1960.

The Old Town was the on the heights. A Royal Mile connected Holyrood Palace with the Castle. St. Giles Cathedral was halfway along the Mile along with the house of John Knox, the Scottish Reformer.

Arthur Reid Thomson grew up in the New Town. Leith Walk led from Princes Street in the New Town down to Leith on the Firth of Forth. Many were the times that Arthur and his brother Alexander sat on the wharf and watched the sailing ships from all over the world.

Dean Ackermann Thomson made a pilgrimage to Scotland in 1998. Dean has determined that the name of Arthur Reid Thomson's father was also Arthur. So he was actually Arthur II.

One tradition has it that King Arthur was enthroned in Edinburgh. A jagged rock formation above the Royal Holyrood Palace has the name of Arthur's Seat. The historic King Arthur was a Kelto-Roman ruler headquartered at South Cadbury in England—Camelot! Coincidentally, Dean Ackermann Thomson's maternal lineage, the Caddy's, came from Kington Magna very near South Cadbury.

On 9 May 1843, Arthur himself embarked from Leith and sailed for America. The Firth of Forth is on the east side of Scotland. They sailed out of the Forth and then northward up around the top of Scotland. The name of his sailing vessel was the *Margaret Bogle*, a three-masted barque of 324 tons built in 1804.

The captain's name was James Morrison. Arthur worked on the ship as a deck boy and thought highly of Captain James Morrison. Arthur's fare was two pounds and ten shillings.

The small barque served a double purpose. It took emigrants to the New World. On the return trip it was converted to a cargo vessel hauling timber back to Great Britain. The rough-cut timber foreshadowed the future of Arthur who would soon train to be a skilled woodsman and carpenter. The returning lumber would be used to rebuild the royal fleet.

Arthur's original intention was to disembark at New York City and then go to Rochester, New York to meet an uncle. The fastest emigrant route into the heart of the United States was by way of the Hudson River to the Mohawk where it merged into the famous Erie Canal near Rochester. The arduous journey through the Appalachian Mountains was thus avoided and newcomers emerged in Ohio and points west.

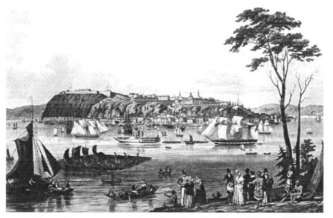

Arthur R Thomson arrived in the Québec City in 1843

During the week ending on 1 July 1843, Arthur Reid Thomson arrived at the Port of Québec. He climbed the steep street to the old city high above the pier where the *Margaret Bogle* was moored. The cafés and hotels clung to the steep ascent.

Less than a hundred years earlier, the Battle of Québec determined the future of the New World even more than the American Revolution. Would the outcome be French or English? Fresh from the Battle of Culloden in Scotland, General James Wolfe led an armada of 49 ships and 9,000 sailors and soldiers to the base of the citadel of Québec City. The French army was securely on alert within the fortification atop the old city. From the shore below, Wolfe and his men looked up at the heights to the massive walls of the stone fort. Scaling that cliff under fire seemed impossible.

If the French had won, most of the heartland of American would have remained New France. Pittsburgh, for example, would have remained Fort Duquesne and not renamed "Pittsburgh" for William Pitt, the British Statesman. French cities like Duluth, Minnesota; Eau Claire, Wisconsin; Pierre, South Dakota; Dubuque, Iowa; St. Louis, Missouri; and of course New Orléans would have remained French.

In the darkness of the night, General James Wolfe led his soldiers silently up the back way. They took the sleeping French army by surprise. The hero, General Wolfe was mortally wounded, but his victory at the Battle of Québec prepared the way for the American Revolution, seventeen years later, in 1776. America would be English.

Arthur climbed the promontory of Cap Díamant of Québec City. Shading his eyes, Arthur viewed the expansive Saint Lawrence River. Far below he saw the *Margaret Bogle*, sails down, nudging the wharf. Perhaps he envisioned the scene a hundred years earlier with Wolfe's fleet of 49 ships, sails unfurled, moving up the river towards the commanding city. Wolfe had dramatically changed the course of American history.[48]

In July 1843, Arthur Reid Thomson made the decision to land at Québec City instead of New York City. Arthur went with the Hutchisons, friends he had made aboard ship during the two-month sea journey. The Hutchisons were destined for Montreal. The Hutchisons were stonemasons. Arthur's father had worked as a stonemason in Bannockburn. The two Hutchison sons followed their father in Montreal. Alexander Hutchison was put in charge of the stonecutting for Christ Church Cathedral when he was scarcely out of his teens. Then he became responsible for the stonework of the entire eastern block of the Canadian Parliament Buildings in Ottawa.

Alexander Hutchison began practice as an architect in 1863 and designed the Hotel de Ville the City Hall of Montreal. He was the architect for Erskine and American Presbyterian Church; being Scottish, Hutchison put his heart into this cathedral church of Scots and Americans in Montreal. Louis Comfort Tiffany came up from New York with stained glass windows. Dr. Gary Arthur Thomson would be the final minister of that congregation before it became part of the Montreal Museum of Fine Arts. The Hutchison stonework and the priceless Tiffany glass still grace the sanctuary that is now a centre for the performing arts.

The European city of Montreal where Arthur Reid Thomson first resided was reminiscent of Edinburgh. At that time Montreal was very much a Scottish city. The banks were Scottish. The

---

48 Dan Snow, *Death or Victory: The Battle of Québec*. HarperPress, 2009. Also the PBS Documentary presented by Dan Snow: *Battle for North America*. http://www.pbs.org/thewarthatmadeamerica/

money that funded the fur trade of the Northwest Company headquartered in Montreal was Scottish. Many street names were Scottish. The book, *How the Scots Invented the Modern World*, was certainly evident in Montreal. While Montreal boasted of being the second largest French-speaking city in the world, at the same time Montreal was also the largest English-speaking city in Canada. In the pleasurable company of the Scottish Hutchison family, Arthur was very much at home in Montreal.

However, Arthur Reid Thomson sought his fortunes west of Montreal where oaks were being cut to refurbish the royal fleet in Great Britain. The lumber was being loaded on sailing barques with three to five masts. Perhaps some of the timbers Arthur cut sailed back to Scotland on a return voyage of the *Margaret Bogle*.

Arthur, raised a city-boy in Edinburgh, began to learn the art of the axe and the skills of rough carpentry. Eventually he acquired the craftsmanship of finely detailed cabinetry. One can appreciate the apprenticeship of Arthur in these formative years 1843-1847 by visiting the *Algonquin Logging Museum*. The exhibition brings to life the story of logging from the early square timber days. One can visualize Arthur astride the top of a giant tree trunk, manning the upper end of vertical two-man saw.

Leonard Nash was a neighbor boy when Arthur was single-handedly building structures on his Homestead. First Arthur cut and close fitted the logs of a cabin. Then granaries, an ice shed, a root cellar, and finally a great house! Leonard said that Arthur was the fastest axe man he ever watched.

At Inverrary, Scotland the Campbell Clan holds Highland Games; the Thomson's are a Sept of the Campbell Clan. One contest is woodcutting with an axe. Too bad Arthur was not there to compete! Inverrary Castle was the setting for the last episode of the third series of *Downton Abbey* on PBS.

In May 1847 at Detroit, Arthur Reid Thomson entered the new Territories of the United States of America. It was a big step in his mind and heart. He was moving beyond the tightly structured society of Queen Victoria whom he had once seen in person at Dalkeith near Edinburgh. With the stroke of a pen, he left the Victorian Age described by Charles Dickens and entered the freer world of American dreams and possibilities.

The Territories of The United States 1850

Michigan became a state on 26 January 1837. The Wisconsin Territory included what would become Wisconsin, Minnesota, Iowa, and the eastern parts of the Dakotas. The Nebraska Territory included Nebraska, Montana, Wyoming, part of Colorado, and the western parts of the Dakotas. Between May 1847 and April 1855, Arthur lived in Michigan and in the Wisconsin Territory. Wisconsin became a state in 1848.

"Arthur lived at least some of his time with the Native Peoples whom he liked very much," wrote Dean Ackermann Thomson. In his book, *Habiru*, Gary Arthur Thomson wrote,

> *The author was born in Nebraska where his great-grandfather homesteaded land that had belonged to Native American tribes for at least 10,000 years. Our history books talked about*

the settlement of the West after Thomas Jefferson purchased the Louisiana Territory from France in 1803 for fifteen million dollars—land that encompassed fifteen current states and two Canadian provinces. We learned about the mail by point express and the coming of the railroad. Settlers acquired railroad land. The Native Americans were the antagonists in the stories. They had a while different life style and concept of property. They had taken care of the Central and Great Plains for thousands of years interacting with the natural environment quite responsibly. European settlers were leery of the natives. When settlers defeated the natives, it was remembered in the history books as a battle; when the natives won the skirmish was referred to as a massacre.

On 5 April 1832, Chief Black Hawk with a thousand Sauk, Fox, Potawatomi, and Kickapoo Native Americans re-crossed the Mississippi River into Illinois in an attempt to reclaim their original homelands. These Native Americans had lost their lands in a disputed treaty signed in St. Louis in 1804. Their return sparked widespread panic among white settlers. A young Abraham Lincoln went soldiering to control this uprising as the settlers called it.

Arthur Reid Thomson trekked into the Wisconsin Territory where the Sauk & Fox tribes were the major tribes in the area at the time. The Sauk, Fox, Mesquakie, and Kickapoo were part of the Algonquian Native People living in Wisconsin. They spoke Algonquian dialects. They are well known for their delicious wild rice. Their sport of *LaCrosse* is like the fast Gaelic team game of *Hurley*. Dean Ackermann Thomson is undoubtedly correct that "Arthur lived at least some of his time with the Native Peoples whom he liked very much."

Certainly later in the Nebraska Territory, Arthur walked alone during the night along the creek banks the thirty-five miles to his homestead. Carpentering during the week in Nebraska City, he would leave after work on Friday afternoon to walk to his homestead. He would arrive early Saturday morning to be with his family. On Sunday afternoon he would begin the return trek to his work on Monday morning. He was following the Native American paths along the creeks. When he met Natives along the way, he would have reconnoitered with them peaceably. A single person alone is no threat. Arthur was an outgoing person not fearful of people; he enjoyed the pleasure of their company!

Dean Ackermann Thomson sleuthed the record of the naturalization process of Arthur Reid Thomson towards becoming a full American citizen. On 2 April 1855 Arthur filed his Declaration of Intention to Become a Citizen at the Office of the Clerk of the Circuit Court of the State of Wisconsin at the Town of Wautoma in Waushara County. By 1 June 1855 his name appears on the Wisconsin State Census as living at Mount Morris, Waushara County, Wisconsin. On 15 June 1855, Arthur purchased 40 acres of land in Waushara County, Wisconsin, Certificate #1004, and again on 15 December 1855, he purchased another 40 acres Certificate #3753.

In the Year 1856, Arthur made an exploratory visit to the Nebraska Territory. The Nebraska Territory was an organized incorporated territory of the United States that existed from 30 May 1854 until 1 March 1867.

On 26 June 1856 Margaret Ronald disembarked in New York City.

UNITED STATES 1854

The Nebraska Territory included lands that would become the States of Wyoming, Montana, a piece of Colorado, most of the Dakota's as well as Nebraska. People and freight traveled in covered wagons drawn by oxen. Long wagon trains of prairie schooners snaked up the hills and down the valleys of this vast Territory of the United States. The Nebraska Territory existed from 30 May 1854 until 1 March 1867 when the State of Nebraska was constituted. Arriving in 1859, Margaret and Arthur Thomson were Territorial Pioneers.

Drawing of Berlin, Wisconsin in 1850 showing House on Grove Street

Margaret and Arthur Go West

"Cruising down the river on a Sunday afternoon!"

Margaret Ronald and Arthur Reid Thomson were married at the home of Andrew and Margaret Christy located at Grove Street in Berlin, Wisconsin on 9 May 1859.[49] The record notes that the house was on Grove Street opposite Basset's Tannery. Dean Ackermann Thomson has discovered this magnificent three-dimensional drawing of Berlin, Wisconsin at that time. Grove Street is named. The tannery is noted. And there is a house across the street from the tannery! And a river flows gently through the town.

---

[49] On 9 May 1843, Arthur Reid Thomson had sailed from Leith, the port of Edinburgh, Scotland..

"Margaret & Arthur were married at 7:00 P.M. on a Monday night and left early Tuesday morning for Nebraska."

"Nebraska!" One could ask, "Why did Margaret and Arthur choose to go to the Nebraska Territory?" Arthur had two farms in Wisconsin. Margaret's immigrant kinfolk were mostly in eastern Wisconsin.

Before meeting Margaret, Arthur Reid Thomson had made an exploratory trip in 1856 to the Nebraska Territory that included Colorado and Wyoming. It was Arthur's recounting of his trip that perhaps gave the couple the vision and the courage to venture forth on a new life together in Nebraska.

Arthur saw the wide-open prairies of the western plains. The tall grass prairie once covered 170 million acres of North America. Within a generation it was plowed under. The prairie sea of grass stretched from the Rocky Mountains to the Mississippi, from the Dakotas to Texas. After the last Ice Age, prairies appeared 8,000 to 10,000 years ago as one of the most complicated and diverse ecosystems in the world supporting an enormous quantity of plants and animals, native grasses and wildflowers, birds and bees.

Uncle Alec often recalled the tall grass prairie. He maintained forty acres of tall prairie grass until his death; then without thinking it was plowed under. Uncle Alec remembered the bluestem and buffalo grass that grew as tall as his shoulders when seated on his pony.

When Arthur Reid Thomson made his first reconnaissance across the Nebraska prairie, he saw a landscape dominated by grasses. Arthur came from Edinburgh where modern science received its impetus from geologists, biologists, botanists, and horticulturalists. Moving along the trail through the tall grasses, he realized that there were many species.

Early botanists determined at least 60 different species of grasses. There were over 300 species of broad-leaved herbs and flowers.

Along the cricks and wetlands, Arthur observed many different kinds of trees and shrubs. In the bottomlands, where a crick bank had washed or broken away, Arthur could see the many strata of soil types of clay and sand, just as James Hutton had observed in the outcroppings on his farm in Scotland. In the niches of a gulch, Arthur inspected wet seeps, sedges and prairie cord grass.

On dry wind-blown hilltops, Arthur saw buffalo grazing on tuffs of hardy quitch grass. He liked the long panoramic views across the wide rolling prairie.

Having crossed the Atlantic Ocean with its vast ecological community of whales, dolphin, fish of every sort, and sea birds, Arthur now experienced the ecosystem of the prairie. The prairie was an ocean of grass often growing taller than a person's head.

A Trail Through The Tall Grass Prairie

Nothing has been recorded of the way Margaret and Arthur traveled to Nebraska. One recollection asserts that "they did not come by covered wagon." An uncle, Claus Rudolf, operated a ferry across the Mississippi for covered wagon travelers at Le Claire, Iowa. Beneath high bluffs, the Mississippi narrows there with flat strands along both sides making the shores accessible. That ferry with its paddle wheel has been maintained as a museum in Le Claire. But we shall assume that Margaret and Arthur did not honeymoon in a covered wagon!

It would seem reasonable that Margaret and Arthur "*left early Tuesday morning*" on a slow boat and honeymooned their way to Nebraska. Steamboat travel was the enjoyable way to go west!

The riverine path from Berlin, Wisconsin to Nebraska City is approximately a thousand miles. The drawing of Berlin shows several steamboats on the local stream that flowed south to the Wisconsin River. The Wisconsin flowed west a hundred miles to where it emptied into the Mississippi at Prairie du Chien. Then, it was 400 miles downriver on the Mississippi to St. Louis and 400 miles up the Missouri River to Nebraska City at the edge of the new Nebraska Territory.

After their thousand-mile honeymoon cruising down the Mississippi and up the Missouri, Margaret and Arthur Thomson disembarked at Nebraska City; this river port was the main passenger and freight depot of the Oregon Trail with its shortened "cut-off" to Fort Kearney.

Ox-Drawn Freighters Moving Through Nebraska City in 1860

Nebraska City had wood block streets at the time. In their first home, Margaret and Arthur operated a small café in relation to the freight depot; Margaret was proprietor of Western House while her husband worked as a carpenter and wagon master.

On 15 February 1860, Margaret and Arthur's first child, Arthur Thomas Ronald Thomson was born in Nebraska City. That was the year of the great fire on the 12th of May. The fire consumed forty buildings downtown.

The 1860 United States Census shows baby Arthur age 3 months, Margaret 27 and Arthur 33. Arthur's occupation is recorded as a carpenter. In addition to his work at the freight depot, Uncle Alec recalled that his father found additional work constructing the new edifice of the Catholic Church.

Mary Artimishia Thomson born on 22 February 1862. That same year on the 4th of April, Margaret was issued a warranty deed to Lot 2 Block 44 in the Prairie City addition to Nebraska City.

Between 1859 and 1865, Arthur worked for the freighting company, Russell, Waddell and Majors—the largest freighting firm on the plains. This company had a contract with the United States Government to move freight and supplies from Nebraska City to Fort Kearney, Denver and Laramie. To be employed by Russell, Waddell and Majors, Arthur had to take an oath:

"I, Arthur Reid Thomson, do hereby swear, before the Great and Living God, that during my engagement, and while I am an employee of Russell, Majors and Waddell, I will, under no circumstances, use profane language, that I will drink no intoxicating liquors, that I will not quarrel or fight with any other employee of the firm, and that in every respect I will conduct myself honestly, be faithful to my duties, and so direct all my acts as to win the confidence of my employers, so help me God."

The original Oregon Trail was plotted in 1842. This initial route divagated north above Omaha and then meandered west along the Platte River.

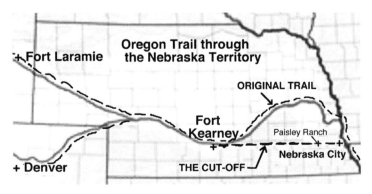

The Nebraska City Cut-Off of The Oregon Trail

Trail makers soon sought a short cut. The Nebraska City "Cut-Off" turned straight west to Fort Kearney. Barges coming up the Missouri River deposited their freight at Nebraska City instead going all the way north to Omaha. The shortened trail literally cut-off a hundred miles for the plodding oxen pulling the wagons full of freight and people. At Saltillo where the wagons cross Salt Creek, the trail makers plowed a furrow to Fort Kearney to mark the way. The new cut-off trail moved ten times more freight and emigrants than the other trails through the Nebraska Territory. Archaeologists like to point out the ruts that still remain from the wagon wheels.

At least once, Russell, Waddell and Majors made Arthur Reid Thomson their Wagon Master. They put him in charge of a freight train of prairie schooners from Nebraska City to Denver. He left Margaret and their two small children in the spring and returned in the fall. In the meantime, Margaret managed Western House in Nebraska City.

Alexander Majors, William H. Russell, and William B Waddell, veteran freighters, added this up river terminal at Nebraska City in 1857. In one season, they transformed Nebraska City from a struggling frontier settlement to a major river port. They bought 138 lots on which they constructed houses, wagon shops, foundries, boarding houses and warehouses. Steamboats unloaded huge quantities of freight to be moved west by ox-drawn freight wagons. Each train usually had twenty-five freight wagons or more. The wagon trains formed lines stretching as long as forty miles! Wagon freighting reached its peak in 1865 hauling 44 million pounds of freight that year. [50]

---

50   James Olson, *History of Nebraska*, second edition. Lincoln: University of Nebraska Press, 1966, p. 106-107.

< Arthur & Margaret Ronald Thomson Homstead #17

Dale & May Thomson Lamb FARM +

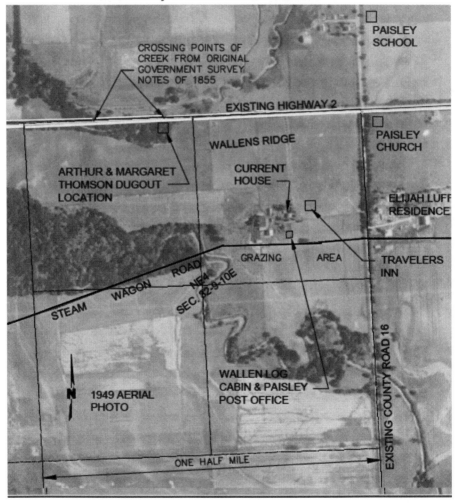

Aerial Map of The Nebraska City Ranch / Paisley Ranch

Survey Notes Paisley – 6 December 1855

Paisley—The Nebraska City Ranch

"Where my caravan has rested, flowers I leave you on the grass!"

The Ranch was the super truck stop of 1862. A string of covered wagons could be seen arriving from the east and another string going out towards the west. The Ranch was busy with selling supplies to the travelers and attending to their needs.

Robert Ronald, Margaret's youngest brother, arrived from Wisconsin and settled in at the Nebraska City Ranch. Robert applied to the Territorial Government to open a Post Office. The officials needed a name. Instead of calling it the Nebraska City

Ranch, Robert called it *"Paisley."* Maybe he was homesick for Scotland and the city he had abandoned.

Folks must have liked the name *Paisley.* Gradually the Nebraska City Ranch took on the name *Paisley.* Later, they added the *Paisley School* and the *Paisley Church.*

The trail also got a nickname—*The Steam Wagon Road.* In Nebraska City a few entrepreneurs like J. Sterling Morton,[51] James Wallen and Arthur Reid Thomson brainstormed the idea of a steam-powered wagon train to replace slow oxen. They believed that a steam traction engine could pull a long wagon train faster across the prairie. Bridges and improvements were added to prepare the way for the famed Steam Wagon that was brought to the Nebraska Territory in 1862. The puffing giant failed, but the route continued to be called the "Steam Wagon Road." The road itself was much better than any of the other trails because it had no sand and it had no large streams to bridge. Like the world's oldest recorded road, *The Icknieldway* in England, this all-weather road followed the ridge ways. With an excellent roadbed, travel was much faster to Denver or Fort Laramie than was possible on the other trails. The road expedited passenger traffic and made faster and better freighting possible with bigger loads. The Steam Wagon Road sustained a greater population expansion and hastened the permanent settlement of the West.

Great Aunt Mary, the second child of Margaret and Arthur, married John Orrison and lived close by the Steam Wagon Road between Nebraska City and Fort Kearney. She wrote:

---

[51] J. Sterling Morton founded Arbor Day—a national holiday observed in all the states on the last Friday in April for the public planting of trees. Arbor Lodge State Park in Nebraska City commemorates this environmental movement that began in the Nebraska Territory.

I see that long string or train, perhaps twenty-five covered wagons each drawn by oxen from Nebraska City.

My mother saw the Old Historic Steam Wagon and my father was among the men who ran it out to the J. Sterling Morton farm where it broke down.

James Wallen, Elijah Luff and Arthur Reid Thomson organized the first major freighter stop on the Steam Wagon Road. Instead of stations spaced 14 miles apart for ox-drawn wagon trains, the puffing Steamer would make 30 miles over the virtually trackless prairie. On the future Steam Wagon Road, the three partners called their freighter pit stop "the Nebraska City Ranch." It would be the first major stop of the mechanized Steam Wagon with its train of freight wagons 30 miles out of Nebraska City.

On 22 July 1862 the Steam Wagon belched its way out of Nebraska City. Loaded at the freight depot on the Missouri River, the monstrous land locomotive hissed its way up the long hill from the river. A forerunner of the railroad, the Steamer pulled a string of freight wagons as far as J. Sterling Morton's farm on the west side of the city. There, unfortunately, it coughed, sputtered and stopped, never to go again!

Fortunately, however, in that same month of July 1862, Abraham Lincoln signed the legislation for a transcontinental railroad, the Pacific Railroad Act. Historians call the railroad the most significant and ambitious American technological feat of the 19th Century. "Westward Ho The Wagons!" The movies conjure up the Wild West where the wagons are circled as an evening encampment along the trail. The Nebraska historian,

A. E. Sheldon, suggests that the Wild West has been greatly exaggerated and lasted less than a decade.

The name "Steam Wagon Road" stuck. The short-cut trail from Nebraska City to Fort Kearney folks named Steam Wagon Road in spite of the fact that the Steam Wagon itself went caput on the outskirts of Nebraska City..

Trains of ox-drawn freight wagons and prairie schooners on the Steam Wagon Road rested their caravans at the Nebraska City Ranch. It was located 30 miles west into the Nebraska Territory.

Arthur Reid Thomson, James Wallen, and Elijah Luff partnered in setting up the Nebraska City Ranch on the Steam Wagon Road. Margaret and Arthur moved to a dugout of the Ranch on the banks of the Little Nemaha where Uncle Alec, William Alexander, was born on 22 July 1864.

On 6 August 1864 Margaret purchased three and one half acres for $21 dollars and 30 cents from Julian Metcalf and F. C. Morrison of Nebraska City. This acreage was the site of their Dugout on the northern edge the Nebraska City Ranch to provide southern exposure to the sun. Like many early immigrant settlers, the dugout was an initial place to live upon arrival. If it were autumn, the new arrivals faced the prospect of the blizzards of a Nebraska winter. Unlike the vertical snowfall of Montreal where Arthur first experienced the New World, Nebraska winds drive the snow horizontally over the prairie and make high drifts of snow. Settlers often tunneled through the snow between their dugouts and the animal shelters. They chopped through ice in the cricks to obtain water.

The dugout could be quickly constructed in a south-facing embankment like a cave. The earth on three sides would insulate the house from the bitter cold. The makeshift door on the warm south side could be opened on a bright day to let in sun and fresh air. On a fierce winter night when it was well below freezing, the door could be draped with sheepskins to insulate the small human abode. The roof had timbered rafters contrived from trees growing near the cricks; leafy branches and straw covered the rafters; finally a layer of grassy sod completed the roof. After the initial rain that eroded soil into the cracks, the sod established a weather proof covering for its human inhabitants.

Great Uncle Alec was born in the dugout on the "sad ranch" as he later described it. He was the third child of Margaret and Arthur. He later wrote about it in the *Nebraska City News Press*:

I was borne in the territorial days. I was borne on July the 27th of 1864 on a ranch kept on the Steam Wagon Road over which freight was hauled by ox to Denver and Fort Kearney and Laramie. The sad ranch was 3 ½ miles due East of Palmyra on Little Nemaha Creek and called at that time the Nebraska City Ranch. This was a place where travelers and freighters took their meals or left sick or played-out oxen to be cared for till the ox trains returned. About the year 1865 or 1866 my father sold this ranch and moved to a homestead 3 miles east and one mile North of Palmyra where he erected a log cabin as that was the typical house in those hard and trying times. In those days people lived as circumstances enabled them to do.

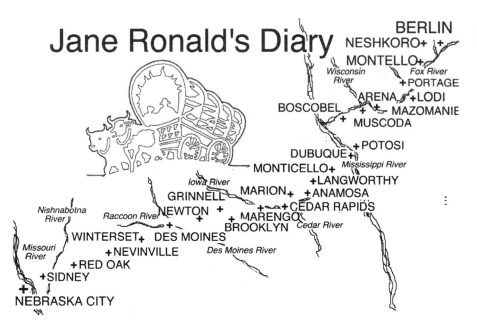

Jane Ronald's Diary

BERLIN
NESHKORO+
MONTELLO+
Wisconsin River
Fox River
+PORTAGE
ARENA +LODI
BOSCOBEL + MAZOMANIE
+ MUSCODA
+POTOSI
DUBUQUE+
Mississippi River
MONTICELLO+
+LANGWORTHY
Iowa River
MARION+ +ANAMOSA
GRINNELL
Nishnabotna River
Raccoon River
NEWTON +
+CEDAR RAPIDS
+ MARENGO
BROOKLYN
Cedar River
WINTERSET+ DES MOINES
Missouri River
+NEVINVILLE
Des Moines River
+RED OAK
+SIDNEY
+
NEBRASKA CITY

This map was constructed on the basis of *Jane Ronald's Diary*—a day-by-day account of her family traveling by covered wagon across Wisconsin and Iowa to the Nebraska Territory in 1864.

Jane Ronald's Diary

"It's an odd idea for someone like me to keep a diary, because it seems to me that nobody will be interested in the unbosomings of a thirteen-year-old school girl."
—Anne Frank, The Diary of a Young Girl

When she saw their caravan while yet at a distance, Margaret Ronald Thomson joyfully ran down the trail to greet them. Her mother, her sister and her brother were arriving after a six weeks journey across Wisconsin and Iowa. Her mother, Mary Ronald was 61 years of age. Her youngest brother, Robert, escorted his family. Her sister, Jane, had been keeping a diary of their journey in the heavy covered wagons as they traveled west in 1864.

The following is that diary excerpted by Dean Ackermann Thomson for the *Des Moines Register* on the occasion of the 125th Anniversary in 1989.

*Left **Berlin**, Wisconsin for Nebraska August 24th, 1864, weather pleasant, traveled till dark. Stopped 4 miles from* ***Neshkoro***, *had to hire pasture, killed and cooked some chicken. Rode all night asleep.*

Thursday, 25th - Traveled from 8 a.m. till 6:30 p.m., made 18 miles. At Neshkoro on white river Maggie (a horse) *got thrown. Robert shot a very large hawk. Stopped in Dutch settlement, water poor, land deserted, and crops worse than our own. Weather good and all well so far. Passed three small lakes.*

Friday, 26th - Traveled from 6:30 this morning until 5:30. Bothered about getting water at noon. Passed five small lakes, three close together, one when we started. Passed through **Montello** *on the Fox about 11 o'clock. The country is worse than when we left, roads knee deep in sand. The wind blew a gale all day. Stopped 12 miles from Portage.*

Saturday, 27th - Started about 8 a.m., traveled a few miles, saw a man that directed us to go via Lodi, Mazimena area and Prairie du Chein. He said we would save 9 miles over Baraboo Hills. We reached **Portage** *about sundown, paid toll on the Plank road, 16 cents for 1½ miles, also came through* <u>Fort Winnebago</u>. *It is a square, built of wood and stone. It is a rickety looking place. It is one-mile north of Portage. Could find no pasture till we traveled about five miles more, when it was as dark as tar. Stopped at a creek, watered the cattle, drove a little further, built a fire, turned out the cattle. Lost the bell. Went to bed. Mother quite sick. Wrote two letters; one to brother William; one to William Bunten.* (Bunten was her future husband who would arrive a year later with her sister, Mary, and her niece, Georgia, in a second covered wagon.)

Sunday, 28th - Found a good pasture, stayed till the afternoon. Killed four chickens, cooked them, greased the wagon, hunted cattle. Tired. Went into <u>Wisconsin River</u> *to bathe. Robert lost his hat. I found the bell. Hitched up and drove three or four miles. Stopped a Scotchman's. Good feed.*

Monday, 29th - Had some homemade biscuits baked at Mrs. McAlister's. She gave us a new loaf of bread and was very accommodating. They came from Glasgow. Started and *drove to a lake, watered the teams. Reached **Lodi** at noon. Robert bought a hat, powder and shot. The roads hilly and rocky. Traveled 15 miles. Stopped in a Dutch settlement. Feed poor. Saw a man at noon. Told us the Indians making great trouble all over. What shall we do! Posted three letters at Lodi. Hills almost perpendicular. The distance between Portage and Lodi, 18 miles.*

*Started at sunrise, Tuesday, 30th - Rode two miles, came to a marsh turned out the teams till 9 o'clock. Hitched up, reached **Mazomanie** about 6 o'clock. Bought a chain, as the cows would break every rope. Traveled two miles out, camped on prairie grass, poor. Had some plums last night, Shot some quail. Lost the kitten. The land in some places fertile, in others poor and hilly. The distance between Lodi and Mazomanie is 22 miles.*

*Wednesday, 31st - Started and drove 4 miles. Reached **Arena** at noon. The roads sandy and poor. The distance between Mazimena and Arena, 6 miles. Iowa County. Traveled 8 miles this afternoon, camped at a creek two miles from **Helena**. Good pasture. 5 o'clock washed a few things. A man wanted to know if Iowa was not full of immigrants already. We drove over 8 miles of prairie this afternoon.*

Thursday, September 1st '64 Started drove two miles through sand knee deep. Reached Helena between 9 and 10 o'clock. It is a city with 4 houses and 1 hog, built on a sand bar. Drove 4 miles more, through ravines and over mountains. Country sandy, hilly and miserable. Oh, dear, I wish I were home again. We are all homesick. Camped on top hill tonight. No water. Will want tonight.

Friday, 2nd – Started, drove down side of mountain. Had to hitch one yoke of the cattle behind in order to keep the wagon from running over the cattle. This makes the third time we have had to do this. Traveled six miles, came to **Avoca**, *travel six more and came to* **Muscoda**. *Traveled over a large prairie, camped, good feed, country sandy in general. Weather pleasant, all homesick. Mother better.*

Saturday, 3rd – Robert very sick, could not drive, so we tried it. We had no water for cattle, so Mother and I drove seven miles ourselves till we came to good feed and water. At noon camped for the day. Robert no better. Mother, Mary and I went up to the top of a very high hill. Never was so high before. Picked some junipers on the top of the rocks over a cave. When we came back we found an ox had eaten all our bread and two pounds of crackers.

Sunday, 4th – It commenced to rain this morning and it has kept on all day. Robert better. Went up to a house a spell, and while we were gone there was a man came to Robert and said we had better drive on about a mile to an empty house, so we started through the rain and here we are all very comfortable. We built a fire in the fireplace and our things are drying. Robert to bed. We had a good supper, plums and hazelnuts.

Monday 5th – Started half past 10 o'clock a.m. Robert better. Drove till nearly 6 p.m. Passed through **Boscobel** *and traveled till night. There was a man told us our best way would be to go to Potosi (crossing the Mississippi at Dubuque). Land very hilly, it seems as though we were going over a range of bluffs all the time. Country better in places. Between Muscoda and Boscobel, 17 miles.*

Tuesday, 6th – Started, drove six miles, came to a guide board that said three miles to Prairie du Chien. Thought no farther than that we would go and get some letters, but we were sadly disappointed. When we had gone three miles, found it was 30, which put us four or five miles out of our way. The country much better here. Camped on a roadside when dark. Turned the cattle into a cornfield. Nothing remarkable occurred excepting a tree fallen across the road.

*Thursday, 8th – Started, drove through **Potosi** without breakfast. Came to the Mississippi, turned out the teams on the river bottoms, pretty well eaten down. Stayed to eat breakfast. Crossed the ferry, paid $1.80. There was a very large steamboat came up as we crossed. Took off my shoes, waded in the river after the breakers. Gathered clams. Started, drove till within two miles of Dubuque.*

*Friday, 9th – Drove through **Dubuque**. It was worthwhile speaking of, it was so much like Glasgow in the main street. It is a very large place. The inhabitants are mostly Dutch. It was county fair, Dubuque County. There was a grizzly bear at one door, stuffed. it looked savage enough. Drove 12 miles. Camped on open prairie. It is rolling and fertile. The grass well eaten down. Land sells for $25 per acre.*

*Monday, 12th – Started this morning early, drove four miles, reached **Monticello**, a small town on the Maquoketa. Met a funeral. There are a great many sick and dying. Came to **Langworthy**. Traveled till night, camped on an open prairie. Had to burn cow manure for the first time. Having an awful time trying to write. It is most dark.*

*Tuesday, 13th — Traveled till noon, came to **Anamosa**. Bought 50-weight flour at $4.50 cwt., one box matches, 10 cents. Traveled within six miles of Marion, camped on prairie.*

*Wednesday, 14th – Well, the cows and oxen got into a man's corn, trod down his buckwheat, ate up his cabbage and dear knows what else. We had to pay the man 50 cents. Started, drove four miles, stopped at a farmhouse, baked biscuits, ate breakfast. Started, came through **Marion** and*

Cedar Rapids, *both about the size of Berlin. Had to pay 60 cents toll to cross the bridge over Cedar River, 30 rods wide. Did not know we could ford it till afterward. Drove seven miles west of Cedar Rapids, camped on open prairie. Hooked some potatoes through a fence. Roads good. Timber very scarce. Prairie.*

Thursday, 15ᵗʰ – Started early, drove till noon, stopped, built a fire, boiled some of our potatoes, ate, drove all afternoon over prairie, came to opening at night, camped with another family coming from Des Moines. They say it is so sickly they were glad to leave, but it is a good market. They have all been sick and are coming back to Wisconsin. There are a great many dying with dysentery and flu. But she told us many yarns we could not believe it all. Gathered hazelnuts as usual. I have eaten so many I have been sick myself for two or three days. O dear, I wish I were a t home again. The distance from Monticello to Anamosa is 16 miles. Between Anamosa and Marion, 23 miles. Marion to Cedar Rapids, five miles.

Friday, 16ᵗʰ – Drove from five miles the other side of Marengo. **Marengo** *is a small place on the Iowa River. We had to ford the river as the bridge was so rickety we could not cross it. Passed a house where there was a funeral. Inquire the price of land of a man, he told me it was from $10 to $40 per acre according as there was timber and improvements. Bought one bar soap. Stopped 11 miles from* **Brooklyn** *on prairie. No wood, no manure to burn. Land handsome, but no timber scarcely. There is a little around Brooklyn.*

Sunday, 18ᵗʰ – The wind blew a gale and cold, traveled until we came to Grinnell, a small town on the railroad. Could find no water till traveled six miles more. Came to a creek, camped with a family going to Nebraska but had had bad luck with their teams so they could not go any further than Des Moines, as they had one horse kicked and bought an old one that was a bad, paid $50 for him. Hired pasture for the other, have to go after him. We washed, dark. Passed five wagons going east, six west. One of Robert's new boots was lost, lost his cap, lost his powder flask in Wisconsin. Robert received 35 cents for one pound of butter. Camped with two Dutch men. Came 17 miles today.

Monday, 19th – Started from the creek, traveled 14 miles, came to **Newton** a village on the prairie, as large as Berlin. No water and no railroad, no conveyance except wagons or stages. The stages run on this road but do not know between what places they go. Traveled three miles more, came to a creek, black water, pump on the roadside, coal miner close by.

Tuesday, 20th – Started early this morning, traveled over the prairie the whole day, came to no towns except one with two houses and six or eight hogs. They keep a good many hogs her. One house had 200. There are a great many sheep, too, passed one flock of 1,000 sheep driving from Michigan going to the western part of Iowa. Camped a spring with a man and his wife who told us big yarns about the Indians.

Wednesday, 21st – Started, traveled 15 miles, came to **Des Moines** about sundown. It is quite a stirring place. You can sell everything you can raise. They say there are 600 Civil War widows in it. I should think there would be a good chance for old batches. Forded both the Raccoon and Des Moines Rivers that was only knee deep. Have to pay toll over the bridge. They say it was never known to be so low before. Camped about one mile out of town. Dark as pitch. No water. Water scarce and poor. Bought candles. From Newton to Des Moines, 35 miles.

Thursday, 22nd – Started this morning early after a wakeful night as the wind blew a hurricane all night and ripped the cover. Drove 16 miles when it came up a thunderstorm. Slept on a man's floor. He charged us two bits. Open prairie. Pasture good. Land worth from $15 to $20 per acre.

Friday, 23rd – Started and drove 17 miles. Passed through a place called Winterset. It is quite a pretty place about as large as Berlin. Tried to get some water for my oxen but could not get a drop and it was sundown and they had not hand any since noon the day before so I drove a half a mile further and camped.

Saturday, 24th – Did not start very early this morning as we were all tired. Backed some biscuits, ate breakfast, had a terrible time with Mary. She will do nothing but as she pleases. I expect we will have to leave here somewhere on the road as she likes to get acquainted with everyone we meet, but won't do anything she is told. Traveled nearly all day without passing a house. Saw the prairie on fire. Wolves thick, crossed a river, camped on the Grand Divide of the rivers, we were on the highest part of the state. The rivers on the east run toward the Mississippi, on the west to the Missouri. I have not been very well for several days. I am dreadfully homesick and the rest are all as tired as I am. Forty acres of land, frame house, barn, fencing on it, good land can be bought for $800. Eight miles from Des Moines. Eighty acres can be bought for $700 five miles from Des Moines. Timber close by.

Sunday, 25th – Drove two miles this morning, came to the Grand River. Camped there all Sunday, stayed in an old frame house at night, cooked some crab apple sauce for supper. Robert talked with an Indian, Potowatomie. He said that we had better not go to Nebraska as the Indians were all joined together from the Rocky Mountains to Minnesota, and they would drive the whites clear back, back. Saw other four but did not speak. I was afraid and could not sleep, wanted to turn back.

Monday, 26th – Started this morning with fear and trembling to keep on our long and dangerous route. We traveled all day over vast prairie without passing a house. Passed 28 dead hogs, one dead horse. Came to a creek, camped on the side of it. It commenced to rain, thunder and lightning and the wind blew a hurricane as it did all day, and ripped the cover off the wagon. So we camped on the ground under it. Spent another sleepless night, cold wet and uncomfortable, as one may suppose. That is traveling, you see.

*Tuesday, 27th – Started this morning cold, wet and muddy, traveled one mile, came to **Nevinville**, a few houses on a vast extent of prairie. Traveled six miles more, missed my Geography, diary in it. Robert went back to Nevinville after it. Also lost Mary's reader. Traveled only 10 miles today. Camped with three men who came from Idaho, who said it is so dangerous where we are going.*

*Friday, 30th – Came to **Red Oak** Junction on a creek or small river. Do not know the names of them all. Bought 25 pounds flour, $4 per hundred, one fine comb, one box matches. Traveled 13 miles more, came to **Walnut Creek**. It rains again. I suppose we must take it as it comes. Robert snapped his gun at a large deer. Saw another dead horse.*

*Sunday, October 1st – Started toward the Nishnabotna River four miles from **Sidney**. We reached the river about noon, camped, built a fire, and had breakfast. It looked like rain in the morning so we thought we would get there before it began. It cleared off a little, so we hitched up again. Did not get far when it began to rain, and blew a hurricane.*

Drove four miles, came to Sidney. It is as large as Berlin before the brick buildings were put up. Camped 1½ miles this side of town on the prairie.

Monday, 2ⁿᵈ – Started this morning without breakfast, traveled three miles, camped, ate breakfast on the prairie, a level tract of country, and 10 miles from the ferry. We came through a range of hills that had the most notched appearance any hills I ever saw. They looked brown when the sun shone upon them. Drove to the ferry, which took us till nearly 4 o'clock in the afternoon. Was ferried across the mighty Missouri on the Boulware Ferry. I did not find it quite so wide as I expected to. It is not quite as wide as the Mississippi. Stopped in **Nebraska City** *nearly an hour. Could find no one who knew the Thomson's. Traveled till dark. No pasture.*

Wednesday, 4ᵗʰ – Started this morning through the rain. Traveled all day, wet and cold. Came to Thomson's about sundown. Was glad to get in and warm and get something warm to eat. Found the folks all well, with another baby addition to the family. John was gone to the Post Office to see if there were letters. Thank God we got her all safe and well.

Uncle Alec was that baby addition to the family. He had been born in the dugout at the Nebraska City Ranch.

After Nebraska City the going was hardly better. The massive freighting wagons of Russell, Majors & Waddell cut deep muddy ruts. The Nebraska City Ranch was a welcome sight to the weary travelers from Wisconsin.

The Freighters Inn was the prominent building at the Paisley Ranch; the structure was 16 x 26 feet with ten windows and three doors; it provided a place for travelers to stay overnight. At the Ranch, as Uncle Alec often spoke of it, travelers could find food for themselves and grazing for their oxen. And the latter fact is probably why it was referred to as a ranch. A stable and corral gave security for the animals. The natural enclosure of the trees and creek surrounding the large meadow offered emigrant ox trains the opportunity to "circle their wagons." [52]

The Colorado Gold Rush of 1859-1860 greatly increased the traffic because the Nebraska City Cut-Off was the best route to Denver. Stagecoaches stopped to allow passengers to eat and refresh themselves. Uncle Alec talked about working at Guss Flootman's store where groceries and general merchandise were sold; it was attached to the James Wallen residence.

Robert Ronald applied to open a U.S. Post Office at the Nebraska City Ranch on 26 January 1869 that he officially named "Paisley." Certainly he was thinking of the city of Paisley in Scotland from whence the Ronald family had come. Gradually the Nebraska City Ranch became known as Paisley Ranch. The stagecoach brought the mail first to J. Randall McKee's place, and from there Thomas Wells brought the mail in his saddlebags to the Paisley Post Office. A second postmaster named Luther Clough took over on 15 July 1869 when Robert Ronald went into the hardware and mortuary business with his brother William Ronald in the new planned town of Palmyra. In rapid succession on 26 October 1869, a third postmaster Edmund Comely was installed who had a homestead nearby. The Paisley Post Office was discontinued on 17 September 1872. These dates are important because they show the rapidly evolving demographics of the

---

[52] Information on the Freighters Inn was taken from the James Wallen homestead papers and from his granddaughter Lucille Wallen.

Paisley community in relationship to the covered wagon trade, the arrival of the railroad, and the progress of settlement in the new State of Nebraska that had supplanted the Nebraska Territory in 1867. Eventually, there remained only the Paisley School and Paisley Church.

Robert Ronald organized the Paisley School #6 in 1869. James Wallen and Elijah Luff gave the land where the schoolhouse was built. Thomas Wells moderated the school board and Fred W. Strachan was treasurer. Miss Lucinda Merwin was the first teacher; she was paid $15 per month. Superintendent H. K. Raymond lived in Nebraska City and walked to Paisley when he made the yearly visit.

The immigrant settlers put a high priority on public, non-sectarian education. Ironically the greatest illiteracy was in New England in the shadows of the Ivy League Universities. A fact that remains true today. The wealthy conservative elite with their exclusive private and parochial schools do not trickle education down to the masses.

In the fledgling community of Paisley, the non-conformist Catholics, Presbyterians, Congregationalists, Methodists and Baptists demanded a public, non-sectarian school to education their children in the liberal values of a democratic society.

William Saunders started the first Sunday School that evolved into the Paisley Congregational Church.

Paisley was truly *a planned village* beside the Nebraska City "Cut-Off" of the Oregon Trail. In the visionary dream of James Wallen, Elijah Luff and Arthur Reid Thomson, the Nebraska City Ranch would be the first pit stop for the proposed Steam Wagon Road. That Ranch became *Paisley!* Like King Arthur's *Camelot,* Paisley for a brief span of Nebraska history was a thriving community of enthusiastic immigrant settlers with high hopes!

Margaret Ronald Thomson's brothers, William and John, had immigrated to America in 1850. They arrived in New York City from Liverpool on the 11th of March 1850 on the *HMS Jamestown*. A decade later, both brothers were in the Nebraska Territory relating to their sister at Nebraska City and subsequently at the Paisley Ranch.

William worked riverboats out of Nebraska City on the Missouri. In 1863 he filed Homestead Application #69 in Section # 32 where Margaret lived at the Nebraska City Ranch. John Ronald also worked on the riverboats and he took a Homestead in Section 32 where his brother and sister lived. John's Homestead application was #356 on 31 October 1864.

In 1870 William became a citizen of the United States of America at Nebraska City. That same year, William purchased the hardware store in Palmyra from Sylvanus Brown. It was the second building constructed in the new village. William enlarged the building and added more variety of stock. His brother, Robert, joined him and they added a mortuary to their establishment. William sold the hardware to W. D. Paige in 1881 and moved to Bradshaw in York County, Nebraska. He died of ailments aggravated by exposure in the Blizzard of '88.

John Ronald envisioned the railroad replacing the Steam Wagon Road. John saw that the future was the railroad that would supplant the ox-team freighting across the plains. John was involved in the measuring and surveying of the railroad right of way from Nebraska City to Lincoln through the villages of Unadilla, Paisley and Palmyra—the old Nebraska City Cut-Off of the Oregon Trail..

Georgia Faye Thomson Bulger, Carolyn Thomson Golden, and Keith Thomson have as their paternal great grandmother, Margaret Ronald Thomson and as their maternal great grandmother, Jane Ronald Bunten. Margaret and Jane being sisters.

Margaret's son, Herbert, was the father of George, the father of Georgia Faye, Carolyn and Keith.

Jane's daughter, Jessie, was the mother of Viola, the mother of Georgia Faye, Carolyn and Keith. So there you have it!

A Native American Burial Mound is located on the Homestead. This mound is at the western edge of the Moundbuilder Culture that extends from eastern Ohio, from Ontario, Canada to the Gulf of Mexico. Native Americans visited the Paisley Ranch and the Homestead. The arrowheads are a collection from the area of the Paisley Ranch.

Margaret & Arthur at Home

Homestead Number Seventeen

"Oh give me a home where the buffalo roam"

Arthur Reid Thomson would be *the seventeenth person to sign up for a homestead.* Arthur signed for the 160 acre homestead on the 8th of January 1863. His partner, James Wallen made the 26th application.

The leaders of the newly formed nation of the United States "in order to form a more perfect union" were keenly aware of their responsibility for *governance* itself. Having forsaken king and a rigid parliamentary party system, the new Americans cultivated a body politic of citizens engaged in a government of, by, and for the people. Public education was mandatory for a democracy to work. A republic ignorant of civics will not stand.

Thomas Jefferson, Alexander Hamilton, Benjamin Franklin and James Madison were all humanists of the 18ᵗʰ Century Enlightenment. They used reason to scrutinize previously accepted doctrines, superstitions and traditions. In 1800 Thomas Jefferson got out his scissors and paste. He carefully took the *teachings* of Jesus from the pages of the Bible and pasted them on a sheet of paper.[53] Like Franklin and Hamilton, Thomas Jefferson was interested in the *pragmatic teachings* of Jesus. Jefferson sought enlightenment from the teachings of Jesus. He is probably the only American President who took the time to translate a few verses from the Greek New Testament each day. The new American mind on the frontiers of the New World took a pragmatic, problem-solving approach to daily life. They were fed up with the ideologies of Old Europe.[54]

Alexander Hamilton and James Madison saw the need for strong *federal governance*.[55] Together they penned the voluminous Federalist Papers to promote the signing of the Constitution. After the war, George Washington wanted to go home. Hamilton could see that the new born country could fall apart. Hamilton rounded up the motley colonies after the Revolutionary War and organized a Continental Congress to write a Constitution. The War debts needed to be paid, so Hamilton picked up the tab for all the colonies and created the first Federal Reserve so to speak. As a result many got rich, but Hamilton lived modestly and died poor.

---

53 Thomas Jefferson, *The Jefferson Bible: The Life and Morals of Jesus of Nazareth*. New York: Beacon, 1989, p. 471.

54 Gary Arthur Thomson, *Parables on Point: Meeting the Mind of Jesus*. New York: iUniverse, 2010, p. 23.

55 Ron Chernow, *Alexander Hamilton*. New York: The Penguin Press, 2004, p. 210.

Thomas Jefferson penned the immortal words that "all men are created equal" but he kept his slaves. Jefferson talked the talk, but it was Hamilton who walked the walk.[56] Alexander Hamilton abhorred slavery. Having grown up in the Caribbean, he knew the atrocities and appalling acts of cruelty inflicted on slaves. Jefferson, the country gentleman, owned slaves and took advantage of his high and mighty superiority. So much for the fine words "all men are created equal." Alexander Hamilton comprehended the plight of slaves. Hamilton wanted the Constitution at its very inception to abolish slavery. But that never happened. It took the bloodiest war in American history to change things.

Jefferson's Vice President, Aaron Burr, met Alexander Hamilton at ten paces in a duel at Weehawken on 11 July 1804. Both fired and Hamilton fell. Burr stayed in his position in the Jefferson administration.

A federal governance was especially needed for *the open lands beyond the Thirteen Colonies* of the new United States of America. Unsettled lands outside the original 13 colonies were often distributed capriciously. Boundaries were established by stepping off plots from geographical landmarks. Land claims overlapped causing border disputes.

On 20 May 1785 the Continental Congress adopted the *Land Ordinance Act* written by Thomas Jefferson. The Act established land policy for western lands until 1862. Jefferson *standardized Federal land surveys*. Using astronomical starting points, territory was divided into a 6-mile square called a *township* prior to settlement. The township was divided into 36 *sections*, each measuring 1 square mile or 640 acres each. To encourage settlement, the

---

56 Jon Meacham, *Thomas Jefferson: The Art of Power*. New York: Random House, 2012.

Government sold half sections of land, 320 acres, for $1.25 per acre. Settlers were allowed to pay in 4 installments.

The most far-reaching federal programs to create jobs and opportunity for all the people came in 1862 under President Abraham Lincoln.

—On 20 May 1862, Lincoln signed the *Homestead Act* to open the west to ordinary people who would work hard.[57]

> *Any U.S. citizen, or intended citizen, who had never borne arms against the U.S. Government could file an application and lay claim to 160 acres of surveyed Government land. For the next 5 years, the homesteader had to live on the land and improve it by building a 12-by-14 dwelling and growing crops. After 5 years, the homesteader could file for his patent (or deed of title) by submitting proof of residency and the required improvements to a local land office. . . . After the Civil War, Union soldiers could deduct the time they served from the residency requirements.*

—On 1 July 1862, Lincoln signed the *Pacific Railway Act.* By May 1869, a transcontinental railroad stretched across the frontier.[58] The new railroads provided easy transportation for homesteaders, and new immigrants were lured westward. The new rail lines provided access to manufactured goods; Montgomery Ward offered farm tools, barbed wire, linens, weapons, and even houses delivered by railroad.

---

57 http://www.archives.gov/education/lessons/homestead-act/

58 http://www.ourdocuments.gov/doc_large_image.php?doc=32

—On 22 September 1862, Lincoln read out the *Emancipation Proclamation* to free all slaves.[59]

After freeing the slaves, the homesteads and the railroads were Lincoln's greatest achievements. Abraham Lincoln accomplished political miracles in 1862.

"That on the first day of January, in the year of our Lord one thousand eight hundred and sixty-three, all persons held as slaves . . . shall be then thenceforward, and forever free. . . .

Abraham Lincoln

The Emancipation Proclamation

After The Battle on The Bridge over Antietam Creek, Abraham Lincoln set forth the *Emancipation Proclamation* abolishing slavery in the United States of America.[60]

But what about slavery in the Territory of Nebraska?

After Thomas Jefferson made the Louisiana Purchase in 1803, Lewis and Clark explored these western lands. They had a black slave named York.

---

59 http://www.archives.gov/exhibits/featured_documents/emancipation_proclamation/index.html

60 After General Sherman's March that ended the Civil War in 1864, Abraham Lincoln was re-elected by the people. And then, then he was assassinated.

The United States Congress enacted the Missouri Compromise in 1820 prohibiting slavery in the lands that would become the Nebraska Territory.

Stephen A. Douglas pushed through the Nebraska-Kansas Act in 1854 dividing the two territories and allowing popular sovereignty to decide the slavery question. Critics said that Douglas compromised the Missouri Compromise. Not thinking about slavery, Douglas was politically concerned that the railroad link between Illinois, Iowa, Nebraska and Colorado be developed. Letting the locals decide the slavery question was his way out.[61]

So, how did popular sovereignty turn out in Nebraska? Franklin Delano Roosevelt authorized a study of the history of the immigration of black people to Nebraska that partially answers this question. The study said,

In the Territory of Nebraska the fight to exclude slavery from within the territorial boundaries spread from the Senate to the press and to the pulpit. Even among the slaves in the South the word spread that here was a place where the attitude toward Negroes was tempered with tolerance.[62]

In Nebraska City there is a log structure near Arbor Lodge popularly called John Brown's Cabin. Allen and Barbara Kagi Mayhew built it in 1854. The cabin was part of the Underground Railroad. It served as a hiding place for black slaves escaping from the South. The cabin had an escape tunnel. Blacks coming up the Missouri River had a "safe house" en route to a new life in the Nebraska Territory.

---

61 James C. Olson, *History of Nebraska*. Lincoln: University of Nebraska Press, 1974, pp. 76-77.

62 Works Progress Administration: "Immigration," *Negroes in Nebraska*, 1939.

Nebraska City must have been something of a hotbed of slavery intrigue. Black slaves were sold at public auction. The Governor of the Nebraska Territory, Samuel W. **Black** favored **black** slavery! He vetoed two anti-slavery bills. Governor Black hedged politically by arguing for popular sovereignty. Some politicians hemmed and hawed that Nebraska didn't need a law because slavery simply didn't exist "in these here parts."

In 1860, Abraham Lincoln appointed Mark Twain's brother Orion to be Territorial Secretary of Nevada. Mark Twain accompanied his brother to Nevada. At that time, Nevada, like Nebraska, was ambivalent and hiding behind popular sovereignty. In *A Connecticut Yankee in King Arthur's Court,* Mark Twain penned "The blunting effects of slavery upon the slaveholder's moral perceptions are known and conceded the world over." And in *The Lowest Animal,* Mark Twain wrote: "(Man) is the only animal who enslaves."

The 1860 United States Census indicates there were 81 black persons in the Nebraska Territory; ten were slaves. The very existence of John Brown's Cabin and the Underground Railroad in Nebraska City raises serious questions.

Alexander Majors had six slaves escape on 30 June 1860. Arthur Reid Thomson worked for Russell, Waddell and Majors between 1859 and 1865. The largest company on the Great Plains moved freight wagon trains from Nebraska City to Fort Kearney, Denver and Laramie. Were Russell, Waddell and Majors utilizing slaves in their freighting operation?

President Lincoln signed the Homestead Act that would go into effect on 1 January 1863.

In Auburn, south of Nebraska City, Daniel Freeman, a Union Army scout, was scheduled to leave the Nebraska Territory to report for duty in St. Louis. At a New Year's Eve party, Freeman met some local Land Office officials and convinced a clerk to open the office shortly after midnight in order to file the first land claim on 1 January 1863.

Arthur Reid Thomson would be the *seventeenth* person to sign up for a Homestead of 160 acres on the 8ᵗʰ of January. His partner, James Wallen made application number 26.

During the summer of 1863, Margaret and Arthur were in the process of moving to a new log cabin that Arthur had constructed on their Homestead.

By June 1864, Arthur had built a log cabin 12 x 16 feet with one door and one window; it had a sod roof. A year later in July of 1865, the Homestead Inspectors arrived. They recorded that Arthur had built the required log cabin. They also reported that Arthur had broken six acres of sod and had planted wheat.

But, he had accomplished far more than that. Arthur constructed a stable, a cattle shed, a log granary, a root house, a root cellar, a corncrib, a rail crib and three hog pens.

Beyond that, in the tradition of Abe Lincoln the rail-splitter, Arthur had also split 80 rods of fence ready to put up.

And if that wasn't enough, the Inspectors went on to state that Arthur had framed a house! They measured its dimensions as 15 x 17 feet. The house was one and one half stories tall. Arthur had shingled the roof with shakes he had split from cedar logs. He had installed a board floor. Interested in details, the Inspectors finally noted that the house was fitted with five windows and two doors.

On 1 August 1865, Margaret and Arthur moved their growing family into their new house on the homestead. Dean Ackermann Thomson has carefully recorded the story.

Dora Margaret Thomson was born 11 January 1866.

Gennia Reid Thomson came along on 9 December 1867 shortly after Nebraska became a state.

John Andrew Thomson was born on 12 February 1870.

On 17 December 1871, Agnes R. McMoreland was born.

In Nebraska City, Margaret's sister, Mary, wed James Thorne. On 8 April 1872 Margaret sold Lot 2 in Block 44 of the Prairie City addition to her sister.

On 1 November 1873, Robert Ronald Baxter Thomson was born.

On 4 May 1875, Margaret and Arthur became charter members of the Presbyterian Church in Palmyra.

That same year on 17 December, Herbert James Thomson, our grandfather, was born.

The United States Census of 1880 records Arthur as a farmer who with his wife, Margaret, have seven children.

On 1 May 1883 Mary wed John Presley Orrison.

On 9 December 1886, Arthur Thomas Ronald Thomson married Ellen Sidles.

On 22 April 1886, Dora married Alfred Henry Wallen.

On 7 March 1887, Gennia married George Daniel Stilwell.

Between 1887 and 1894, Arthur and Alec operated Thomson Brothers Butcher Shop in Unadilla.

Tragically, their first-born, Arthur Thomas Ronald Thomson died on 05 March 1894. Arthur became legal guardian for his daughter in law Ellen and the three minor children Nellie, Charles and Hazel.

On 6 December 1905, our grandparents, Herbert James Thomson and Blanche Mabel Klinefelter were married at Pittsburgh, Pennsylvania.

On 9 May 1909, Margaret and Arthur celebrated their Fiftieth Wedding Anniversary. Arthur died on Christmas Day 1913.

As this book is written, 150 years have passed since Arthur and Margaret made application for their Homestead. The land remains within the Thomson family. Dean Ackermann Thomson is now the owner of the Thomson Homestead.

Family of Dean and Elida Thomson

Family of Arthur Thomas Thomson & Ellen Sidles
Thomson with Charlie, Hazel, and Nellie

Alec Thomson in 1904

Uncle Alec & Charlie

Ever Living God by whose mercies we have come
to the gateway of another year, grant that we
may enter it with humble and grateful hearts.

And confirm our resolutions, we beseech Thee,
to walk more earnestly in Thy way according to
the teaching and example of our Saviour thy
Son Our Lord. And forgive us for the sins and
offenses of the past. Pardon us and set us free
that we may serve Thee with a clearer conscience
and a better hope. And gird us by Thy Spirit that
we may walk in the path that leads more and more
unto that perfect day of our Lord and Saviour
Jesus Christ.
—A Grace given on New Year's Day
by Uncle Alec

Well dressed in suit and tie on most occasions, Uncle Alec stood tall with a signature white mustache. Ninety-something, he signed as W. A. Thomson for William Alexander. A country gentleman in every sense, he was the venerable patriarch. It was understood that he would offer the grace at gatherings like Thanksgiving and New Year's Day. Always present when work was being done on his farm, he watched with a century of horticultural experience. Alec was born in a dugout in the Nebraska Territory during the Civil War. He grazed cattle on the aboriginal prairie watching the changing seasons. In the late 19th Century, the heyday of American public transportation, he had traveled the length and breadth of North America on the new railroads. When one talked to Uncle Alec, you were respectfully aware of his critical appraisal; he listened with empathy to what you had to say before engaging in conversation.

When you visited Uncle Alec in his big house he would often be resting on his leather Chaise Longue—a reclining chair with a long seat that supported his outstretched legs. His great grand niece, Lorraine Thomson often visited him; he lived just down the road. She now has this Chaise heirloom.

Uncle Alec would rise to greet his guest and offer a chair beside his cumbered dining room table. Letter and papers were informally yet neatly placed on the tablecloth. The letters of Georgia Graham, his cousin in Oregon illustrated his correspondence. Today we email on the Internet and twitter 145 characters. In the great English and American tradition of letter writing, Alec spent many hours weighing his words that reflected meaningful relations with many people. He lifted a letter and read a descriptive paragraph about the Oregon seashore. Georgia's husband, Arnold Graham was involved with the fisheries of Oregon & Alaska.

Charlie Thomson was a transitional figure between the older generation and the new. Charlie's father was Arthur Thomas Ronald Thomson. Margaret and Arthur's first-born—Arthur Thomas Ronald Thomson—died tragically at the young age of 34 leaving a young wife and three small children—Nellie, Charlie, and Hazel. The children grew up listening to the stories of the era of the covered wagons. Nellie, Charlie and Hazel became storytellers themselves.

Charlie and Ruth lived in the smaller house hardly twenty feet from Alec's big house. Charlie had the *Thomson General Trucking* business; Ruth managed the small two-pump gas station—one for gasoline and the other kerosene. A gurgling crick snaked around the corner plot where the two houses stood at the northeast periphery of Palmyra, Nebraska.

Gary Arthur Thomson published an anecdotal story of Charlie in his doctoral thesis:

When the author was a boy he often traveled with Charlie in his stock truck to take cattle to the Omaha Livestock Exchange. The afternoon began by making pick-ups from various farmers. R.R. Miller had three steers. Joe Dowding had an aging milk cow. The author's dad had four year-old bull calves. At Merle Severe's' we picked up a dozen steers and we had our load.

Charlie was a likeable gregarious person. He chewed tobacco and would spit before he began his latest story. By the time we had rounded up the load, the author had heard the story four times and each time the story got better.

Halfway to Omaha we would stop at the Louisville Café. Everything stopped with the arrival of Charlie. The waitresses refilled coffee cups and paused to listen. Charlie knew them all by name. Here the story assumed epic proportions. Everyone was in stitches when Charlie motioned that we had better be on our way.

Like the Seven Hills of Rome, the stockyards covered the seven hills of South Omaha. Pens and more pens full of bawling livestock. Our cattle truck lumbered into the main gate and we were directed to the scales. It was a ritual known well to Charlie. All the commission men, dealers and buyers, recognized him as we made our way closer to the chutes. At the scales Charlie told his tale one more time while the agents took charge of unloading, weighing and assigning our cattle to the inner precincts of the market. The commission man was laughing at Charlie's latest joke, as he pressed down hard with his pencil. His marks went through three layers of paper with interlinear carbon sheets—one for the Exchange, one for Charlie, and one for himself.[63]

---

63 Gary Arthur Thomson, *First Market: The Genesis of Wall Street in Ancient Iraq* (New York: iUniverse, 2010, p. 139)

When Charlie was only six years old, his father had died. Born on 15 February 1860, Arthur Thomas Ronald Thomson passed away on 25 March 1894. He left his wife, Ellen, and three children—Charlie, Nellie, and Hazel. His "father-figure" became his grandfather, Arthur Reid Thomson.

Charlie was born 30 October 1887. Charlie grew up watching his Scottish grandfather and listening to his stories. The man who had emigrated from Scotland, resided in the metropolis of Montreal, lived in the woods for a time with Native Americans, teamstered ox-drawn prairie schooners across the prairies, opened a truck stop on the Steam Wagon Road, and built a Homestead at Paisley—that eclectic man became Charlie's mentor and closest friend.

They say "like father like son." If that is even partially true, then knowing Charlie we can infer something about the personality of Arthur Reid Thomson.

Uncle Alec, it is said, supported his mother, Margaret. Alec was a little boy tugging at her skirts in the log cabin. Alec was still a baby when his parents moved from the dugout at the Nebraska City Ranch at Paisley to their new log cabin a mile northwest beside Hooper Crick. The English gridiron roads had not yet been surveyed.

One of his first memories was of his mother pulling in the latchstring on the door of their log cabin. Somebody was outside. Native Americans often padded silently by along the crick. The Natives had a burial mound near the cabin. From the Ohio River Valley west, archaeologists have identified over 2000 mounds from the time of the earlier Moundbuilder Culture four thousand years ago. But young Alec knew his parents did not fear the Native

Americans. The problem arose from gangs of ruffians encamped at the Nebraska City Ranch. The ruffians were out looking for some mischief to amuse them. Log cabins of nearby homesteaders were vulnerable prey to their vandalism. By the next day, the ruffians would be on their way taking their pleasure in bull-whacking their slow oxen on the Oregon Trail.

Every weekend the little boy anticipated his father coming home after a week of carpentry in Nebraska City. Early Saturday morning as the sun was rising in the east, his mother would be outside the cabin with breakfast prepared on the table her husband had hewn from nearby timber. Then his dad would appear coming through the trees. He had walked all night to cover the thirty miles from Nebraska City. He would be with them until Sunday afternoon when he donned his backpack full of clean cloths to begin the return trek.

Alec, his parents, his older brother Arthur and his older sister Mary, and his baby sister Dora were all Territorial Pioneers as they were later feted. His siblings who arrived later were born after Nebraska became a state in 1867.

When Margaret worked in the store on the Nebraska City Ranch at Paisley, Alec toddled beside her. Later, Alec and his brother, John, had a general store in Unadilla. When their father died in 1913, Alec and John built a new big house in Palmyra where they lived with their mother, Margaret, until she died in 1927. So, perhaps, we may infer something of the graciousness of Margaret in the gentlemanly character of her son, Alec.

Charlie would have imbibed the stories of Arthur Reid Thomson wagon mastering an ox-drawn freight caravan from

Nebraska City, to Fort Kearney, to Denver, and to Fort Laramie. A thousand miles in 14-mile increments adds up to a hundred encampments. The details in the stories piled up of thundering downpours of rain, flooded cricks and sloughs. Add to that, the storyteller continued, there were muddy trail ruts, disabled oxen, and broken axles. And one cannot forget the prairie fires, out-of-control, bearing down on the vulnerable wagon train. Little Charlie was bug-eyed with astonishment. Oral tradition grows more fantastic with each re-telling.

Charlie and Ruth Thomson

Charlie grew up to be a new kind of cattle drover. In his time, Omaha became the largest livestock market in the world, Chicago being a close second. Omaha was the market junction at the end of cattle trails. After that, Omaha became the hub of the Union Pacific and Burlington Railroads.

Like his entrepreneurial grandfather and grandmother, Charlie started a trucking business. He liked his Jimmies, his GMCs. Charlie's son Roy became his chief mechanic to keep the fleet of trucks rolling.

Nellie Thomson married Ora Baker, a handsome farm boy from Iowa. After farming for a while in Otoe County, Nellie and Ora moved on to Brady, Nebraska. Eventually they settled in Wyoming where they raised their family.

Hazel Thomson married Frank Hoyt and lived in McCook, Nebraska. Their son, Cloyd, is alive and celebrating 95 years. Frank was prominent in the Equity Grain Cooperative in Nebraska, often serving as president of the company. In McCook, Hazel and Frank were neighbors of Senator George W. Norris, the progressive Republican Whip of the United States Senate during the time of Franklin D. Roosevelt. Norris cooperated with Roosevelt in the New Deal. Norris helped to set up the CCC—the Civilian Conservation Corps that built roads, bridges, and buildings. This work employed thousands of people seeking jobs when America was coming out of the Great Depression. Norris worked with Roosevelt to provide Social Security for all Americans, a safety net. They were also cooperating to create a universal health care program. George W. Norris, in that incredible era, spearheaded universal electrification of all rural America, the REA. Norris was the force behind the Tennessee Valley Authority to provide navigation, flood control, electricity generation, fertilizer manufacturing, and economic development.

Back home in Nebraska, George W. Norris was part of the initiative to build an architecturally magnificent state capitol paid in full when completed. As a progressive Republican in Nebraska, George W. Norris crossed party lines to develop the non-partisan Nebraska Unicameral Legislature. Interestingly, Scotland has recently followed the Nebraska model; Scotland has now developed the most representative legislative assembly in the world. Even the softest voice is heard.[64]

Hazel and Frank Hoyt were keen to write the history of life in the Nebraska Territory. Like Charlie and Nellie, her mother and her grandparents had raised Hazel. She remembered stories of the first cabin near the creek that was still standing when Hazel was a child.

This cabin was built of logs grown on this farm, personally cut and hewed by Arthur Reid Thomson. The logs were hewn flat on the inner side and notched to fit at the corners. To make the logs fit down as closely as possible, all small openings were filled with hay and clay mixed together. A chimney was composed of the same mixture. The roof was first covered with split logs about three inches thick, and covered with prairie sod then by a layer of clay to make it water proof. It never leaked after the first rain that settled the earth together. The floor was Mother Earth the first year, and then Grandfather got some more poles, and laid them for floor joists. He laid some rough boards over them for a floor.

This cabin was 12 x 16 feet. Along the east side were shelves on which was a clock and matchbox. A bureau stood beside the shelves. Against the north wall stood the cupboard with table close by. The four chairs when not in use were pushed up against the table. Two large wooden trunks, which contained clothes, were pushed under the beds. Every inch of space was continually in use. On the beds, a feather mattress lay over good bright straw; then sheets and blankets and quilts. Two

---

64 George W. Norris, *Fighting Liberal: The Autobiography of George W. Norris.* New York: Macmillan, 1945.

children were born in this cabin, Dora Thomson Wallen and Gennia Thomson Stilwell. The family resided in this cabin for six years and moved into the frame house about 1869.[65]

The frame house appears later in the Christmas recollections of Glenetta Bunten, daughter of Margaret's sister, Jane.

They had a nice little sitting room which had a bay window alcove – a dandy place for a Christmas tree. This room was connected with a large living room by double sliding doors and with the dining room….We celebrated Christmas with dinner always bountiful that there was enough of us for the table to be set a second time…Then in the early evening the doors into the sitting room would be closed and everybody gathered around the room to await Santa Claus and the gift distribution. The little folks would usually be too full of expectation and excitement to notice that one of the men was missing. We were Charlie, Nellie and Hazel Thomson, James and Arthur Wallen and Jimmy Stillwell and myself. If anyone mentioned the absence of Uncle George, the explanation was that he had to milk the cows. We were always awfully sorry that he'd had to miss the festivities. We would hear a jingle of sleigh bells and before long Santa would come in the front door greeting everybody jovially, He seemed a bit near sighted so one of the women would read the names to him as she passed him the gifts to distribute.

New Years was always a happy occasion – checkers, dominoes. The boys, Alex, Johnny and Herb were always good about playing with us. In the late afternoon we often gathered around the old organ to sing.

---

[65] Frank and Hazel Thomson Hoyt, *Hoyt-Robenmyer & Thomson-Sidles Genealogy & Early History.*

My father and Uncle Arthur always spent their time together in lengthy discussions. Both were readers and kept abreast of the news. Both were a little hard of hearing and each eager to put his point across so voices were often raised. On one occasion, these two men, one with the carving knife and the other with the stove poker were brandishing them as they talked.(Aunt Dora motioned for us) to come and look. (We all) burst into hearty laughter. When it was called to their attention that they had been brandishing lethal weapons they laughed as heartily as anybody.[66]

Ellen, the mother of Nellie, Hazel and Charlie, was a Sidles. The Sidles' owned the Buick dealership in Lincoln, Nebraska.

Uncle Alec drove a big, black 1936 Buick with a massive straight-eight overhead valve engine. He pointed out the many luxurious features of the Body by Fischer—fancy running boards, little crank-out vent windows, upholstered seats. Every Sunday, Uncle Alec drove the Buick to the Presbyterian Church where he always parked in the same place. He would come early and sit in his Buick until others arrived.

One day Uncle Alec took us in his big black Buick to John Mahoney's Lumber Yard in Palmyra. Dramatically, Mr. Mahoney unlocked the door to a room at the back of the store. Uncle Alec motioned us in. There at the side of the large room was parked a shiny 1913 Buick. Uncle Alec explained that our grandfather, Herbert James Thomson, had purchased it new. He went on to say that it was the very first electrically lighted automobile sold by Sidles Buick. The car was a posh green color. The gearshift was mounted on the door.

---

66 From the pen of Glenetta Bunten, daughter of Jane Ronald Bunten.

Blanche and Herb had three boys by 1913 to ride in the back seat—Alexander, Arthur, and Alfred.

Uncle Alec was an Elder in the Presbyterian Church in Palmyra where his Scottish parents had been charter members when the congregation came into being. "Presbyterian" derives from the Greek word for *elder*—presbuteroi. Elected by the people, ruling and teaching *elders* governed the church. Desiring liberty and freedom, Presbyterians did not like kings or bishops. Scottish Presbyterians had been prominent in the American Revolution; King Georg III had called it "the Presbyterian Rebellion;" the English Prime Minister, Horace Walpole, said, "Cousin America has run off with a Presbyterian parson." The Scots had turfed out the exclusive, secretive Masonic Order. Elected elders like Uncle Alec were required to be open and transparent. Congregations had to be *inclusive*! Whosoever will may come! Nobody is turned away or blackballed!

The Presbytery of Nebraska City elected Uncle Alec to represent them at the national General Assembly of The Presbyterian Church USA. Like a responsible senator, Alec read through the mountain of amendments to be voted on. Some of those documents still remained on his dining room table.

For a person born in a dugout, Uncle Alec was extremely literate like his parents. When he was a boy grazing cattle on the aboriginal prairie, Alec was not just sitting there chewing a straw. He was more likely to be reading a book!

Occasionally, when he stood up to stretch, he sang! The prairie meadow listened to his songs. In the evening, Alec might go to the Stilwells', the Wallens', or the Nashes.' His teenage friends got together to hang out and sing! With no piano, they sang in the living room of a log cabin. Socializing, the young people sang *square note songs*. Tuning up, they vocalized: *do, re, mi, fa, sol, la, ti, do*. In the traditions of Medieval and Renaissance music, these prairie youth sang *a capello* by candlelight. They sang in unison and sometimes they harmonized. They sang both homophonically and polyphonically in rounds. It was remarkable self-entertainment. There were no couch potatoes in this youthful society.

So, now and again, when young Alec was grazing cattle, he would stand up and belt it out: *do, re, mi, fa, sol, la, ti, do.*

And then with prairie chickens and coyotes for an audience, Alec might sing a ballad by Robbie Burns that his mother had taught him:.

O my love is like a red, red rose that's newly sprung in June
O my love is like a melody that's gently played in tune.

Alec was a baritone.

Alfred, Arthur and Alexander with a motley mix of Irish Catholics, English Methodists and Scottish Presbyterians attended Grandview Public School where church and state were separated. At Grandview, the democracy envisioned by Abraham Lincoln worked itself out pragmatically with tolerance. Parochial and private schools were frowned upon because they carried the ideological baggage of the Old World with its enslaving class systems and religious intolerance. The teacher was Alma Clark.

Aunt May

May Thomson Lamb and Alma Thomson Caddy

Here it is Spring again and the birds are singing;
grass is growing and flowers are blooming!
The trees have taken on their Summer garb;
the plumb trees are just white with bloom;
and the lilac, cherry and apple trees as well!
—Uncle Alec to Georgia Graham, 5 May 1919

May Thomson Lamb, Alma Thomson Caddy, and Faith
Thomson Nash were the daughters of Blanche and Herb.

Aunt May lives on her farmstead near the site of the Paisley
Schoolhouse with her daughter Janet. Her second daughter,

Deanna, works as a criminal lawyer in Los Angeles. The television series *LA Law* comes to mind. Aunt May resides a short distance from the Paisley Corner where stood the Paisley Church.

Ancestral voices sing from the Paisley Corner and The Nebraska City Ranch where Margaret Ronald and Arthur Reid Thomson lived in a dugout. That dugout first home is also just a short walk from Aunt May's farm. A mile to the west is the original Homestead #17 of Margaret and Arthur. The Homestead has remained in the Thomson family; Dean Ackermann Thomson presently holds title. The farm of Aunt May and Uncle Dale Lamb adjoins those lands.

R. R. Miller was the Headmaster of Palmyra High School when Blanche and Herb's children were educated there. Robert married Louise Jones and they settled on the Jones' family farm that contained the site of Grandview Country School #85. Blanche and Herb's children were enrolled in elementary school at Grandview. The Thomson Homestead where Blanche and Herb now lived was a little more than a mile across the fields to Grandview Schoolhouse. A motley mix of Irish Catholics, English Methodists and Scottish Presbyterians attended Grandview where church and state were separated. At Grandview, the democracy envisioned by Alexander Hamilton and Abraham Lincoln worked itself out. The immigrant settlers who built Grandview Schoolhouse placed it on a summit of land surveying a panoramic view of the surrounding countryside. Truly a "grand view!"

Louise Jones Miller was a pianist. Folks referred to her as "Mrs. Miller." Every Sunday at the Palmyra Presbyterian Church, Louise played an inspirational classic by Bach, Schumann, Beethoven, or Brahms. Verna Wall Thomson created a choir of 35 young voices to sing praise to God each Lord's Day accompanied by Mrs. Miller.

Robert and Louise decided to will their farm to Cedars Home for Children. They moved the Grandview Country Schoolhouse into the yard of their farmstead. Their dream was that children could come and visit an early country school. The school was furnished with desks and blackboards and ticking clock. The Millers passed on to their eternal reward and the farm was bequeathed to Cedars. A self-assured new manager at Cedars with an MBA in greed arrived on the scene. He called in the volunteer fire department and invited the community to come and watch "the burn." The farmstead of Robert and Louise Miller with the Grandview Country Schoolhouse went up in smoke to be replaced by profitable cornfields! The orphan children at Cedars never got to visit the country school. Arthur Klinefelter Thomson whose early education was in the Grandview Schoolhouse hastened to retrieve the ticking clock from the inferno. Mrs. Bill Beacham lived across the road from the Miller farmstead. Arthur and Verna escorted Mrs. Beacham to their home for the evening so that she would not have to watch the fiery spectacle of the Miller farmstead and schoolhouse. And so it goes.

During World War II the sons of Blanche and Herb each farmed parcels of the Homestead. Their youngest, Reid, who tinkered with the farm generator and Atwater-Kent Radio, went off to war in the South Pacific fleet. Reid was the Radio Operator on the destroyer, *USS Quick*.

His brothers cultivated Reid's farm where the Native American mound was located.

Reid's son, Barry, would graduate from the Technical High School of The University of Nebraska and become a fine cabinetmaker, carrying on the woodwright traditions of *Spessart Oak!*

In those early war years, Alexander, Arthur, Alfred and George still shucked corn with wagons drawn by teams of horses. Big Red, the Nebraska Cornhusker Football Team got its name from the days when corn was husked by hand in the field. A special leather strap with a hook fastened over one glove to husk the leaves away from the hard ear of corn. Then the ear was thrown against the backboard alongside the 25-bushel wagon box and onto the growing pile of corn ears. The wagon box was cradled between four very tall wheels that were easier for the team of horses to pull. A "tchex-tchex" sound from the corner of the farmer's mouth would signal the intelligent horses to move forward a few steps. Ear by ear, row by row, the corn was garnered from the field. Four loads of corn totaling 100 bushels was a good day's work. Each load was scooped up into the crib at the farmstead. The rich bottomland of the Homestead sometimes produced 100 bushels per acre.

In the early hours on the east forty, we could hear Uncle Dale singing in the clear morning air from his adjoining farm. There were no tractor engines to drown out the sounds of nature. A diverse chorus of birds mixed their chirps with the cackles of crowing roosters. Now and again a cow would bawl out to its calf to add the symphony of early morning sounds. The steady staccato of hard ears of corn banging into the wagons gave a rhythm to the pastoral scene.

Dale sang tenor.

From One Generation to Another,

we dedicate this book to

our wives, our children and their spouses,
and our grandchildren

Elida Esther Angulo Thomson
  Paul Dean Thomson
  Daniel Alfred Thomson & Martha Joan Hier
    Joseph Daniel Thomson
    Elena Frances Thomson
    Hannah Elida Thomson
    Emma Louise Thomson
  Sharon Elida Thomson & Todd Christopher Kosta
    Logan Scott Kosta

Jeanette Antonette Kroese Thomson
  Kimberly Ann Thomson & Nigel Dove
  Shannon Adele Thomson & Charles Ellison
    Sionna April Ellison
  Jill Andrea Thomson & Bruce Wright
    Calla Jeniken Wright
    Griffin Garrison Wright
    Maya Lindsay Wright
  Dawn Antoinette Thomson & John Nugent
    Jess Reilly Nugent
    Amelia Francis Nugent

The Family of Dean and Elida Thomson

The Family of Gary and Jeanette Thomson

Index

Lightning Source UK Ltd.
Milton Keynes UK
UKOW041314260513

211221UK00001B/72/P